TERRIERS

THEIR TRAINING, WORKING & MANAGEMENT

By

VARIOUS AUTHORITIES

TERRIERS

Their Training, Working & Management

THE AIREDALE TERRIER

Top. THE RT. HON. T. K. LAIDLAW'S SOMERTON SOLARIO (DOG)
Bottom. MRS. BANES CONDY'S HUCKLEBERRY HARMONY (BITCH)

TERRIERS

THEIR TRAINING, WORKING & MANAGEMENT

Edited by A. CROXTON SMITH

With Contributions by
Capt. Banes Condy, Baroness Burton, Capt. L. C. R.
Cameron, R. Clapham, A. Croxton Smith, Walter S.
Glynn, The Hon. Mr. Justice Hanna, K.C., Count
V. C. Hollender, L. Irwin Scott, Fred W. Lewis,
N. A. Loraine, W. L. McCandlish, Duchess
of Newcastle, Major G. B. Ollivant,
Mrs. Cyril Pacey

With 36 Illustrations showing both sexes
of each breed of Terrier

CONTENTS

CONTENTS

LIST OF PLATES

CHAPTER ONE

RATTING WITH TERRIERS

By *CAPTAIN L. C. R. CAMERON*

A FORMER Duke of Beaufort is reported as having said : " There are only two sports : Fox-hunting and Ratting : and Ratting is a damned good second " and even to-day there are sportsmen who will be inclined to agree with this dictum. When frost or fog confine hounds to kennels then is the time to have out the terriers, call upon the ferret court and put in a couple of wintry afternoon hours in killing off in sporting style some of the numerous small vermin that infest stable and granary, barn and byre, pig-stye and stackyard.

A really good terrier of almost any breed will kill rats with gusto ; but those that enter most quickly and are keenest and most easily handled are the " working " type of English Fox Terrier, both smooth-haired and broken-haired, the Highland Terrier—now known to show bench fanciers as the " Cairn Terrier ", the Border Terrier, and the diminutive but most sporting Yorkshire Terrier. Bull Terriers, Bedlingtons, Kerry Blues and even Airedales will all kill rats after a fashion ; but the smaller, handier breeds are most to be recommended, if sport as well as slaughter is the aim and object. The famous " Billy, indeed, who used to kill rats for a bet " was, I believe, a Manchester black-and-tan terrier of sorts, a breed now infrequently seen.

Time was when every little town in England boasted its " sporting publican," and every sporting publican owned a rat-pit. And a rat-pit, of some sort, is essential for entering a terrier to the game if he is to kill his quarry gamely and cleanly. Few terriers will do either until a rat has given them a nip that they can remember to the end of their days. A ratting terrier should be entered at six months old, at latest, by being dropped into a pit with at least three buck rats, when his future value in life will be quickly estimated. Of course, any terrier that has been entered to fox, otter or badger will kill a rat as soon as, or sooner than, look at it.

Rats, unfortunately for the national exchequer, but fortunately for owners of terriers, abound everywhere in Great Britain ; and there should be no difficulty in getting a day's sport in any month of the year, or in any part of the country.

Except when corn is being threshed ferrets are a necessary adjunct to terriers in killing rats, and every dog employed must, of course, be thoroughly broken to ferret, which is quite simply to be done. Taking terriers to a rick-yard during threshing operations is, however, not recommendable. All sorts of curs and mongrels are usually assembled there, accompanied by undisciplined youths and men armed with formidable sticks. They will often make a cut at a fleeing rat regardless of the proximity of the dog, with the lamentable result that a valuable terrier is blinded, or even gets its back broken, or at the best is " broken from rat " for ever.

The invariable rule where terriers are taken ratting must be that no one should carry a stick. If anyone wearing trousers is afraid lest a rat should run up his leg,—as they have been known to do—let him put a pair of 'cycle-clips or a piece of string round his ankles and leave his stick at home.

The most sporting form of ratting with terriers is to be obtained at ricks in the open fields, such as are to be found in Wiltshire, Berks, and other Southern Counties. The ricks should be surrounded by owners holding their dogs, while the ferrets are put in at the top of each rick. The rats will speedily vacate it, some leaping from the eaves, while others work down through the corn until finally driven out in a crowd by the descending ferrets ; when the fun will be fast and furious as the rodents streak for an adjacent rick or the nearest hedgerow.

I have a record of nearly 800 rats being killed in this way in two days' sport on a Wiltshire farm just before the war by a team of Fox Terriers belonging to a well-known New Forest hunting man. There are few out-lying ricks on any farm that are not after November tenanted, much to their detriment, by colonies of rats.

Before that date, according to the season, rats will be found in most hedgerows bordering arable fields or those bounded by wet ditches. The best way to ferret these hedges is to work them up to a gateway, where a man with a good dog is to be stationed. Those rats that do not try for safety over the open, giving other dogs their chance, will race across the gateway to the farther part of the hedgerow. When the ferrets have worked up to the aperture they should be taken to the far end of the unferreted hedge and worked back to the gateway, where the stationary terrier will have another chance at them. Hedges unfrequented by rabbits are the best for the purpose, and a mild still day should if possible be chosen. On frosty or wet and windy days the rats will not bolt readily, and the ferrets are disconcertingly apt to lie up and require digging out.

Ratting in stables, barns, and outhouses is rather a chancy proceeding. It is difficult to know whither the ferrets go, or to guess precisely where the bolting rats will appear—and disappear. Partitions, mangers, bins and lumber hamper the terriers and facilitate the rats' escape. It is at best a *pis aller* for a wet day. If, however, rats infest a pig-stye it is not a bad plan at dusk to carry a terrier quietly to the place and pop him suddenly over the wall, when he will quite probably kill a brace or a leash before all of the rats can escape. The dog will generally require a bath in some deodorizer before being taken indoors again.

CHAPTER TWO

WORKING TERRIERS FOR FOX AND BADGER

By MAJOR G. B. OLLIVANT

FIRST of all make certain that you have the sort of terrier whose build will enable him to do his job efficiently and with ease to himself. In addition to the right conformation it is absolutely essential for the terrier to possess good pluck, nose, voice, endurance and intelligence, for these are all indispensable in his work. The terrier's pluck must not be the bravery of the Bull Terrier that goes in regardless of consequences, but the brave, fearless kind of pluck that knows its own danger, and yet has the grit to stay there. Therefore grit and pluck must come before every other consideration. Unless a terrier has a good nose he is unable to tell quickly if an earth is occupied, and should it be occupied he must at once get up to his quarry and use his voice, throwing his tongue continuously. As a terrier may have to stay up against his quarry for a long time on end he requires plenty of staying power. While as for intelligence, he requires that all the time.

When being worked to fox it is the duty of the terrier to drive the fox out of an earth as quickly as possible, but if the fox happens to be a hunted fox, this may not be easy, for he has gone to ground for sanctuary and to save his brush from hounds, so, being a cunning varmint, he knows that it is better to stand up to the gallant little fellow in front of him, rather than face hounds again by bolting into the open. This is the time when a terrier is apt to get into trouble and receive punishment, for a bad-tempered old dog fox is a nasty customer to tackle, and though a terrier must go in and endeavour to make the fox bolt, he must not be too hard and kill, or get killed himself. He must be plucky in the attack, but his pluck must be backed up by brains, and he must know equally well when to retire and throw his tongue. The terrier should learn that he must only give tongue when the quarry is at home, and must not be a babbler

20

and make a noise simply for his own pleasure when an earth is empty. Should an earth be empty he must come out at once and say so.

If a certain amount of trouble is taken in the early training of a terrier, it is well repaid later on. In the first place it should be taken as a general rule that no terrier should be entered to either fox or badger before he is eighteen months old, though preliminary training may take place considerably earlier, for it is advisable to bring the puppy on gradually. A start may even be made when the whelps are with their dam. Put a few pipes in their run and cover with a little earth to make things look more real, and the puppies will soon find their way into the pipes, either in play, or to get cover from the heat of the sun, or again a bit of meat or a bone may be pushed into the pipes as an inducement for the puppies to enter and find the food. In this way a puppy will become accustomed to going to ground and turning in a narrow space, until he thinks no more of going through a drain or earth, than he does of going through the stable door. It is well to have pipes of different sizes to accustom a terrier to going into all sorts of places, and when he is accustomed to the larger ones he can be put into smaller and tighter places.

Those who wish to have their terriers really well trained, will probably have an artificial fox earth made near ground level where they can easily get at the pipes. When the puppies are big enough they may be allowed to chase young rats through the pipes and watch their mother kill them ; though don't put puppies at a rat when they are too young, and never at an old buck rat until they are well grown and thoroughly accustomed to killing young rats, for should one be badly bitten at the start it is liable to put him off. Now comes a more difficult thing to arrange, and it may not be possible to manage it, but if it can be worked try to accustom the young entry to the scent of their quarry, and get them to connect this scent with an earth or drain ; and just in case a fox should happen to be available, pass him through the pipes or artificial earth, and *immediately* you have taken up the fox, put the mother of the puppies down at the earth and let her puppies, or some of them, follow her through the earth. The bitch will show keenness when she gets the scent of the fox, and will infuse keenness into her puppies so that they will become just as keen themselves when they come to work alone. Should the bitch not have been properly entered herself, some other trained terrier will have to show the way in her place.

I always consider that terriers must tell each other their past experiences, for I cannot think that an animal who can make himself understood to human beings has no means of communicating with his own species. Therefore, I like to put an old well-tried veteran amongst the youngsters, for they must gain by it, and my experience has been that they have benefited by it, in the same way that I did myself when a youngster. A good old sportsman, whether dog or man, must have a good influence on the young idea. When the terrier is approaching the age of eighteen months old he may be taken to see how the veterans work at either fox or badger, and perhaps he will learn a few tips from them. It is advisable that the youngster should not take any active part himself the first time that he is out, but he will see the other terriers at work and get accustomed to the surroundings. Advantage should always be taken of occasions such as this to give the young entry a real good worry at any kill. Slip the terriers both entered and unentered, and let them all have a good worry while you drag the dead body away from them. The young entry will quickly copy the old-stagers, and lay hold in the general excitement of the worry, which will teach them to connect up and recognize the scent of the quarry, with the scent of their quarry on future occasions when they catch his scent under ground. When the time comes for the terrier to be entered, try and enter him on a quiet day when there is nothing to distract his attention or upset him ; and have your best terrier with him to show him what to do. In training a dog my experience has always been that there is no better way of teaching the young idea, than by having a well-tried veteran to show the youngster what to do and how to do it.

I will now deal with make and shape. Each breed of terriers has its admirers, and without going into the conformation of the various terrier breeds, I will give the best conformation suitable for work both above and below ground, and leave the reader to decide for himself where these points differ from some of those of the recognized terrier breeds. Though the same build of terrier can be used for badger as for fox, there are certain requirements in a terrier that is worked to fox which may not be absolutely necessary in one used solely for badger, and though my remarks on conformation apply equally to terriers for badger they must be taken to mean the stamp most suitable for a Hunt Terrier under all conditions. I take the Hunt Terrier as the best example of the standard of work required for work to fox.

A very necessary thing in the management of the Hunt Terrier is transport, or the means of getting a terrier to an earth as soon after the fox has gone to ground as possible. Hunts manage their terriers in one of the following ways :—

(*a*) By letting the terrier run with hounds, in which case he must have the activity and endurance to keep up with hounds, or I should say as near to them as he can manage to get.

(*b*) Another way is for the terrier to be in charge of the Terrier Man. This is not so hard on him as running with the pack, but an active terrier is required nevertheless. Some Hunts put their Terrier Man on a bicycle which makes it easier for the terrier, as he gets a lift by being carried in a bag or basket on the machine.

(*c*) Other Hunts carry the terrier in a bag in front of the saddle of a Hunt Servant. Obviously a small terrier is easier to carry than a large one, but there is no reason why a small terrier that is carried should not be active.

(*d*) Lastly, terriers are carried in motor-cars, which of course is the easiest of all for the terrier. We must not lose sight of the fact that a Hunt Terrier has to be got to the mouth of an earth before he can start work underground, therefore an active terrier is very necessary while in addition to his day being a long one, he must always be ready at any time to face his fox underground, and bolt him.

It is difficult to lay down any hard-and-fast rule as to which terrier is the most suitable in all cases, for the conditions in different hunting countries vary, while on the top of this each M.F.H. has his own individual likes and dislikes about the type he uses, but unless we evolve some suitable conformation, just as a basis, that will meet the majority of conditions we don't get any forrarder, and working terriers will never breed true to type, but just remain nondescript, while the result of any breeding operations will be entirely due to chance, and so no definite type of shape will become fixed.

I can make my meaning clear by explaining that the conformation I like, and the conformation I have always found the best for a Working or Hunt Terrier is that which approaches the nearest in build to the short-backed short-legged hunter ; a terrier will then be able to do the dual work required of him in the most satisfactory manner and with the greatest activity and comfort to himself. *Like the short-legged hunter he must have long, well-laid-back, sloping shoulders, a short back, and big long galloping quarters.* This conformation will make him stand over a lot of ground, in spite of the fact that his back is short and not long. Though size and conformation not up to this standard may be used in some countries, the short-legged hunter type of terrier is suitable for practically all countries.

I have found that a certain stamp of show-bred Fox Terrier takes a lot of beating for work when properly entered, but he must have the make and shape of the short-legged hunter. When dog show people call a show terrier a working sort of terrier they are apt to include terriers that I, at any rate, would not pick out for a Huntsman's Terrier ; but if a show terrier conforms in build to that of the short-legged hunter, *and some of them do,* then one is getting along on the right lines.

It is not my object in this chapter to crack up any particular breed above any other breed of terrier, but I have mentioned the Fox Terrier, and when I say Fox Terrier, I mean show-bred Fox Terriers with the necessary working points, simply because they possess, and are bred for, so many of the good working points that are required in a working terrier. For instance, they are bred for good neck and shoulders, a very necessary point in a working terrier ; they must not be too wide in the chest, another good working point ; bone, legs, and feet are all points most carefully bred and highly prized in the show Fox Terrier, and which are all sound working points. A show terrier should not be straight in the stifle, neither should a working terrier ; hocks should be well let down, and the quarters should be big and muscular, points that a working terrier should also have, while last but not least show terriers must have good, true, level action, which is a most important point for any terrier that has to get about a country, and has to carry out the duties of a Hunt Terrier. If these points belong to a terrier whose conformation is that of the short-legged hunter, then you have a great deal towards the make up of a working terrier, at any rate as far as the conformation is concerned. I have previously dealt with grit and pluck, and have stated how absolutely essential they are. A terrier that has to work under-ground must have his heart in the right place ; then if his body permits him to do so, he will get there like the good sportsman he is.

Many huntsmen and private individuals who work their terriers have their own particular strain of terrier which can trace back for several generations of good working blood. These terriers are bred almost entirely because their parents are working terriers. Other points are not generally taken into consideration at all, except perhaps the keeping down of size. The result is that many of these terriers are nondescript, and many of them have certain points of their build which are a handicap to them when they are at work, though their pluck and working sense are good. Great admirer as I am of the pluck and work of these terriers, I cannot help feeling that they could be vastly improved, and given a conformation more suitable for work, if only they were bred to terriers such as I have previously described, either by mating a working bitch to a show Fox Terrier dog, or vice versa, but the show terriers used must be of the long, low sort built like a short-legged hunter. This is very important. It must always be remembered that the good working points of show Fox Terriers, such as sloping shoulders, legs and feet, etc., are not just due to chance, but have been bred for for many generations, and this fact will make it more than likely that these points will be reproduced again. To breed certain working points into working terriers that will improve their conformation, and prevent them being handicapped at work by faulty build, we *must go to blood where these points have already been stamped for generations*, so that they will be reproduced. Therefore, one must use show Fox Terriers for this purpose as there is no other source available, but I must emphasize the fact once more, only use show Fox Terriers that are of the short-legged hunter type.

Many people complain that show Fox Terriers are too long and narrow in the head, and that as a result must lack brains, though I don't think this has ever been definitely proved, either one way or the other, and given the proper environment most terriers will be found all there. Unless one is specially breeding for long narrow heads there is not much likelihood that long narrow heads will crop up amongst one's terriers, for these are points that breeders of show terriers are striving to stamp, but so far they have not been able to do this with any degree of certainty, and many good winning show Fox Terriers are regularly criticized by show people, because they are too short in the head and too thick in the skull. Long narrow heads do not as a rule occur as a matter of course in breeding, unless they are specially bred for, and are more or less a modern fancy point that has not yet become definitely fixed. Therefore heads always revert back to the original type if left alone, so use show Fox Terriers for their many other good qualities, and you will not get long narrow heads if you don't want to breed them. Another point to remember is that *nearly every show Terrier gets thick in his skull before he is two years old*, so we must not give them credit for a point that they do not necessarily possess except perhaps as youngsters, while even so they are helped out and made to look narrower than they are by excessive trimming. I think many people forget this, or perhaps they are not aware of the fact.

Too long a jaw does not appear to be the most suitable for work, but one can easily go to the other extreme, and I have seen working terriers both too short and too weak in the jaw. Loss of jaw power is a serious fault in a working terrier, so one must not go to extremes in either direction or be too faddy either way. A medium length of jaw would appear to be the most suitable for tackling a fox or badger, and one that is broad near the nostrils will give the firmest grip. It is considered by many people that too long a jaw does not get the best grip, and that a terrier with an overlong jaw is slower in laying hold, and easier to shake off, than one with a shorter and broader jaw. Nevertheless, by far the best terrier I ever owned for work was a show Fox Terrier, and he had a long jaw, and, incidentally, a lean narrow skull, and yet he was simply teeming with brains. All of which goes to prove how difficult it is to dogmatize on a thing we cannot ourselves see.

The JAW of a terrier for work must be a really strong one, the TEETH must be long, strong, and level, and the nostril big. COATS must be weather-resisting and as hard as possible, with a good undercoat. Personally I do not like a long rough coat as it holds wet and dirt, and myself prefer a hard, flat, tight coat, for it seems to me to give greater protection, though the Bull Terrier type of coat is most unsuitable in every way.

I have mentioned some of the good sound working points that can be obtained from show-bred Fox Terriers, and if a small dark eye, small ears, and good tail carriage should also result, though not specially bred for, they are points that will certainly not do a working terrier any harm, but will help to smarten him up; and I see no reason why a good-looking terrier should not also be a good working terrier, if his conformation is right for work, and he is a good plucked 'un.

It is customary to talk about the Jack Russell strain of terrier, though Parson Jack Russell never bred any particular strain of working terrier. Any terrier that was dead game was taken into his terrier pack, and provided it filled his eye, that was the one and only qualification required. Besides, it is rather ridiculous to talk nowadays of any strain of terrier which is supposed to have existed so many years ago, when the owner of that particular strain has himself been dead for nearly fifty years. Why, any strain would have *ceased to exist as such long ago*. When people of these days talk about the Jack Russell strain, I suppose what they really mean is a terrier descended directly either in tail male or tail female from one of Parson Jack Russell's terriers, which is not quite the same thing. Parson Jack Russell owned some very game terriers, and it is interesting to note that a very large number of show smooth Fox Terriers are directly descended in tail female from his good bitch Judy (1868), or Juddy as he called her.

It may seem strange to advocate show-bred terriers for work, but unless they are used either wholly or partially when breeding working terriers, important working points cannot be obtained and fixed, but it is a pity when show people pure and simple obtain the control of any breed of dog, even though they may improve working points, for the control of any breed should not be in the hands of those who will not work their dogs.

The great difficulty in breeding hunters is because there is no specific breed of hunter. Most hunters are bred from chance-bred mares by thoroughbred sires, and it is the thoroughbred sire, because he has been kept thoroughbred, that holds them together. This is why I am advocating the use of show Fox Terriers of the short-legged hunter type to improve the working conformation of the working terrier, and because certain sound working points have already been fixed in show Fox Terriers for generations. Those who already have working strains of their own may prefer to keep to their own working terriers, but I hope that some of them at any rate will try my suggestion.

My own preference for work is a small show-bred smooth Fox Terrier of the short-legged hunter type, and I have never known them fail me when properly entered, but they must be small, and of the long low sort with short back, built like a short-legged hunter.

CHAPTER THREE

TERRIERS

THE AIREDALE TERRIER

By CAPTAIN BANES CONDY

NO book dealing with Sporting Dogs would be complete without mention of the Airedale Terrier, the largest and hardiest of the whole terrier family.

One occasionally hears people say that to call him a terrier is wrong as he is too big to go to ground. I have in my paddocks, where the Airedales exercise, burrows from seven to ten feet long into which they disappear into the bowels of the earth, and made entirely by their digging for an imaginary quarry to amuse themselves. It comes naturally to them to go to ground in search of something.

Of course it is not possible for an Airedale to get down a fox-earth, but against any animal his own size that goes to ground he immediately proves his terrier characteristics by going after him, and this must be so when one realizes how he was manufactured about seventy-five years ago. He will always tackle or hold an otter or badger.

Little did those old Yorkshire sportsmen who invented him dream that he was going to be so improved as to become the most popular dog in the world. Why is he? Why is it that wherever you go in town or country I should say that on an average about one in every four dogs you see is an Airedale. It is because as a one-man dog he is unsurpassable, because he can be trained to do anything that it is physically possible for him to do. The man or woman who lives in the country and wants a sporting companion and protector will find him delightful as such, affectionate, good tempered, faithful to people he knows and especially devoted to children, who can romp and play with him without the slightest danger.

I remember many years ago when my son was a baby he was put out on a fine warm day on a rug on the tennis lawn to amuse himself. While there, an old dog named Huckleberry Hector (whom we used to call " Toddy ") strolled up with a huge bone in his mouth, laid down on the lawn beside the child and chewed it. The baby crawled over to him and took the bone out of his mouth. My wife and the nurse saw it from a window and were horror-stricken, but the dog gave it up without a murmur and sat and wagged his tail at the child with it. Splendid guard of person and property he is. My sister-in-law when she was married went out to live in Northern Rhodesia and took a couple of Airedales with her for protection. They lived 50 miles from anywhere, and when her husband was away she was often left quite alone with Kaffir Boys. On one occasion one of these boys commenced to grin and move towards her, so she warned him if he came any nearer the dog would have him. However, he pressed forward and the dog sprang at him and sent him flying off.

If his master or mistress likes going out with the gun he is in his element as he has a keen, sensitive nose, and is a born hunter and vermin killer, especially from water.

He adapts himself to nearly any climate, is bold and courageous and therefore has been used for all kinds of sport throughout the world. He is hunted in pack in India after jackal, where his good nose, hardihood, lasting capabilities and strength make him invaluable. I have exported many for the purpose, and marvellous accounts I have had of their prowess.

In the western part of the United States and Canada he is greatly used for hunting the brown and grizzly bear, and is claimed to be the only breed with the necessary gameness, grit, and staying power for the sport ; moreover, he soon learns the finer points of the game, and shows natural aptitude for it. When tackling a bear he shows the marvellous headwork and discretion which are so necessary. Of course everyone knows how successful he has been as a War and Police dog ; also at life saving and Ambulance work, but this is not the place to discuss that part of his adaptability.

He is an excellent water dog and can enter the water at nearly all times of the year, when most others would refuse.

He is easily trained to retrieve from either land or water, and can be taught to beat game from a rough cover. He can also be taught to drive cattle and sheep, and makes an excellent farmer's dog. With very little trouble he will learn to hunt the trail of either man or beast.

Before I further dilate on his sporting merits perhaps it would be interesting to let you know something about his origin, and why it is he so readily adapts himself to water or anything to do with it. Coming as he does (and there is no question in my mind about this) from the old English Black-and-Tan Terrier that was used so much in the 'seventies for rat hunting matches, which were so prevalent and popular on the banks of the River Aire in Yorkshire, and the Otter Hound (generally the former was the sire and the latter the dam) it is no wonder that anything appertaining to water attracts him, and he is in his element. His sensitive nose and swimming and diving capabilities come of course from the Otter Hound.

As a retriever from water he is perfection. I once sold a puppy to an old friend, a retired sea captain, who went to Ireland to spend his retirement in indulging in his pet hobby, duck-shooting. He told me that he had never seen such a wonderful retriever from water as this Airedale ; he became quite notorious and was borrowed for duck-shooting by people from all parts. The good nose, hardihood, love of hunting from water of the Otter Hound, have evolved one of the most useful dogs available. I have mentioned that there is a natural instinct to guard and protect, and a case that was brought to my notice the other day is remarkable. How it was reported to me was because the Airedale concerned was by a dog in my Kennels out of a bitch from my Kennels. It was at Hayes, Middlesex, when a man got away from the local bank with £100. The dog was let loose and held him up in a field until he was collared. That dog had not been trained at all ; it was the protective and hunting instinct exemplified. I am sorry to say that in discussing the breed with so many people I often hear it said that an Airedale is quarrelsome and is a fighter. Let me disillusion everyone at once from an experience of forty years with Airedales. He is not quarrelsome, and will never seek a quarrel, but if challenged he is always ready to take his own part and often to administer chastisement, for he is built on fighting lines and nearly always can hold his own against most. Is it not recorded of the famous Crack that he defeated the great champion bull terrier that had never been beaten ?

Symmetrically he is a thing of beauty as the adjoining photos will show, and recently one of his breed has on several occasions won the coveted special prize for the best dog or bitch of any breed at several of our biggest championship shows. .

One point I should like to accentuate. People, both breeders and novices, have somehow or another got it into their heads that an Airedale must be a rich black-and-tan in colour. This is erroneous ; a light tan and grizzle back is just as correct provided the coat is hard in texture. In fact, it was the usual colour until quite recently.

The HEAD should be long, SKULL flat, but not too broad between ears, narrowing slightly to the eyes, free from wrinkle. STOP hardly visible, and CHEEKS free from fullness. JAW deep and powerful, well filled up before the eyes. LIPS tight.

EARS V-shaped, with a side carriage ; small, but not out of proportion to the size of the dog. Black NOSE. EYES small and dark in colour, not prominent, but full of terrier expression.

NECK of moderate length and thickness, gradually widening towards the shoulders, and free from throatiness. SHOULDERS long, and sloping well into the back ; shoulder blades flat. CHEST deep but not broad.

BACK short, strong and straight ; RIBS well sprung. HINDQUARTERS strong and muscular, with no droop ; HOCKS well let down. TAIL set on high and carried gaily, but not curled over. LEGS perfectly straight with plenty of bone. FEET small and round, with good depth of pad.

COAT hard and wiry, and not so long as to appear ragged. It should also lie straight and close, covering the dog well all over the body and legs. The COLOUR of the head and ears, with the exception of dark markings on each side of the skull, should be tan, the ears being of a darker shade than the rest, the legs up to the thighs and elbows being also tan. Body black or dark grizzle.

THE BEDLINGTON TERRIER
By HAROLD WARNES

This terrier, which is British throughout, can be traced as a distinct breed for nearly two centuries, and originated from Bedlington, a village in Northumberland whence it derived its name. He has always been a favourite with the miners, principally owing to his wonderful gameness and fearlessness.

The earliest authentic record we have of the Bedlington is of a dog named Old Flint, who was owned by Squire Trevelyan and was whelped in 1782. The descendants of this dog have been traced in direct line to 1873. The standard of points of the Bedlington, as adopted by the National Bedlington Terrier Club, is as follows :

SKULL narrow but deep and rounded ; high at the occiput and covered with a nice silky tuft or topknot.

MUZZLE long, tapering sharp and muscular ; as little stop

as possible between the eyes so as to form nearly a line from the nose end along the joint of skull to the eyes. The LIPS close fitting and without flew.

EYES should be small and well sunk in the head and not too wide apart. The blues should have a dark eye, the blue and tans dark with amber shade, the livers and sandies a light brown eye. NOSE large, well angled ; blues, and blue and tan should have black noses ; livers and sandies flesh coloured. TEETH level or pincer-jawed. EARS moderately large, well formed, lying flat to the cheek, thinly covered and tipped with fine silky hair. They should be filbert shaped. LEGS of moderate length, not wide apart, straight and square set, and with good-sized feet, which are rather long.

TAIL thick at the root, tapering to a point, slightly feathered on lower side ; 9 inches to 11 inches long and scimitar shaped.

NECK and SHOULDERS. Neck long, deep at base, rising well from the shoulders which should be flat.

BODY long and well proportioned, flat ribbed and deep, not wide in chest. Slightly arched back, well ribbed up with light quarters.

COAT hard with soft undercoat, and not lying flat to sides.

COLOUR dark blue. Blue and tan. Liver. Liver and tan. Sandy or sandy and tan.

HEIGHT about 16 inches.

WEIGHT, dogs about 24 lb., bitches about 22 lb.

GENERAL APPEARANCE. He is lightly made, lathy dog, but not shelly.

The Bedlington is a fast and enduring dog, equally at home on land and in water. He will work an otter well, draw a badger or bolt a fox, and nothing can touch him at rats or any such vermin—he is very intelligent and sagacious, and can be trained to retrieve. In short, he is the handy man of the canine race.

The Bedlington has frequently been used with foxhounds and otter hounds with excellent results, being fast he is very useful for rabbit coursing and has been known to push up and catch a rabbit in the open and occasionally a hare.

They should be trained when quite young. All that is required is firmness and patience, and gaining their confidence. This is very essential, for many of them are of a nervous disposition and likely to become cowed or broken-hearted if afraid of their master, but once their confidence is gained they can be taught anything. They are very quick to learn what is wanted of them, and seldom if ever require a thrashing,

THE BEDLINGTON TERRIER

Top. MR. WARNE'S CRANCE JIM (DOG)
Bottom. MR. H. COX'S JILL OF MOTTISFONT (BITCH)

unless it is for a very serious fault. They are very sensitive, and if spoken to sharply when doing anything wrong they will quickly desist, will wear a worried look and become dumpy until spoken kindly to, for to get out of their masters' good books completely upsets their equanimity. They are really human in this respect, resembling a child that is being scolded, but they are always anxious and ready to make it up and never sulk. If one bears in mind these traits in their character the training of Bedlingtons to one's own ways and tastes should be an easy matter—always remembering to gain and keep their confidence.

They are easily broken to ferrets, and can be trained to hunt hedgerows equally as well as spaniels.

Like most terriers they are prone to hunt on their own, and be away for hours on end. This propensity is very difficult to cure unless it is stopped at the outset, but this, of course, only applies to a dog that always has his liberty.

Frequently when puppies they will kill fowls, but this habit can easily be checked. Cats are the natural enemies of the Bedlingtons and care should be taken to break them of the habit of chasing and killing cats, which they are very likely to acquire, and if not nipped in the bud the habit is likely to become a nuisance to the owners and an annoyance to his neighbours.

If brought up properly and kept under control and taught obedience they make perfect companions, being very affectionate, faithful and highly intelligent.

Their fighting propensities, which are certainly inherent, can easily be stopped when they are young as they are very quick to learn what their masters disapprove, and if checked will give up the habit and never begin a quarrel with another dog, but if attacked they can take care of themselves, and in most cases render a very good account of themselves. This applies more to fighting with dogs of other breeds, for it must be admitted they are fond of a scrap with one of their own brethren in which case sex seems to make no difference for a dog and bitch will quarrel just as readily as two of the same sex. Their quarrels always originate from jealousy, as they are of a very jealous temperament, and when once two Bedlingtons have had a fight they never seem to forget it, but are ready to go for one another at the first opportunity, and even when they have not met for a year or two they still remember their ancient feud and begin their battles over again. A great deal can be done to prevent this by stopping them at the outset and by

c

avoiding the possibility of their quarrelling over bones, the
most fruitful source of their rows.   When they do fight they
mean business and punish one another terribly, never uttering
a sound once they have started, and if not separated they will
continue until they are exhausted or one is killed.   They never
give in once they begin, for they do not know what fear is.   To
give an idea of their pluck, there is an authentic record of a
young dog twelve months old being put to a fox's hole to try
him, but he could not kill the fox.   The owner then stupidly
put in the young dog's father, who not being able to reach the
fox actually killed the young dog and then reached and killed
the fox.

There is also on record a story concerning a dog named
Piper who belonged to a Mr. Ainsley in about 1820 ; he was
set on to a badger when eight months old, and from that
time until he was fourteen years old was constantly at work
more or less with badgers, foxes, foulmarts, otters and other
vermin.   He drew a badger after he was fourteen years old
when he was toothless and nearly blind after several other
terriers had failed.   I heard from a Bedlington breeder recently
of a dog who was frequently killing hedgehogs, and yet would
carry a hen's egg in his mouth without breaking it.

The Bedlington is hardy and healthy, with any amount of
energy and endurance, and is, if properly trained, in every
sense a sporting terrier.   He has gained considerable popularity
on the show bench of recent years, due in a large measure to
the number of women who have interested themselves in the
breed.   Thirty years ago a dozen specimens at the few shows
that catered for them was considered a very good entry ;
nowadays they may exceed 100 entries at shows like Crufts,
the Kennel Club, etc.   Also in the eighties and nineties one
could buy a pedigree one for 30s. to 40s., now there is a good
demand for them, puppies making from £5 to £10, and
prize-winners anything from £20 to £100.

For the man who has only one dog the Bedlington is
unrivalled as a real " pal ".

THE BORDER TERRIER

By A. CROXTON SMITH

About the only criticism that can be levelled against Border
Terriers is about their colour, which may occasionally lead to
disaster through hounds mistaking them for the fox, and

mauling them badly before the error is discovered. If they are kennelled with the hounds such a thing is not so likely to happen, and it is only right to say that some Masters consider the risk is so slight that it need not be worried over. Beckford, in his *Thoughts on Hunting*, expressed similar apprehensions, though he was thinking less of the hounds than of the followers. " I should prefer a black or white terrier : some there are so like a fox that awkward people frequently mistake one for the other." That sporting parson, the Rev. W. B. Daniel, repeated the warning a little later in almost identical language. " Terriers to run with hounds should be rather large, although in an earth their size may not always permit them to get up to a fox. The black or red-and-white are to be preferred, those that are altogether of a reddish colour awkward people may mistake for a fox."

The padre's preference for a bigger terrier to run with hounds would not be endorsed generally to-day, most Masters liking them smallish. Size, within limitations, does not seem to impair their activity, as the Borders are smaller than most fox terriers, yet they are able to get thereabouts when they are wanted without being carried in a bag on a horse. Most people like the Borders to be about 15 lb. in weight, and in one or two hunts they are as light as 9 lb. or 10 lb. The standard framed by the Northumberland Border Terrier Club for the guidance of show judges puts the WEIGHT of dogs at from 13 lb. to 15½ lb. and bitches 1½ lb. less. Membership of this club is restricted to residents in the Northumberland and Border Hunts, and it was promoting local shows before the little dogs were introduced to a wider public. In 1921 they had a show at Rothbury at which thirty-seven competitors appeared in a single class. Although they were being talked about enthusiastically before the War, it was not until 1920 that they were admitted to the registers of the Kennel Club, from which we may assume that they were then beginning to appear at ordinary shows. Some of their supporters predicted that they would soon be among the most popular of the show terriers, but this anticipation has not been fulfilled, much to their advantage many sporting men will say. Whether showing is detrimental or otherwise will always depend upon the class of men who take up a breed. Personally, I have a preference for good looks either in dogs or horses, and so long as the points are not exaggerated no harm need be done by trying to improve the appearance.

I am a strong advocate of preserving breed type, and I am

glad to see that most of the Border Terriers one meets bear
unmistakable evidences of the racial character. Though this
volume is concerned most with working qualities it is not out
of place to describe the kind of dog that breeders want. When
Border Terriers first came on the show bench there was the
possibility that ignoramuses might have aimed at the produc-
tion of a small Irish Terrier, although, as a matter of fact,
there is no similarity between the two.

The standard of the Northumberland Border Terrier Club
explains that the HEAD should be shaped like that of the otter,
the SKULL being flat and wide. The JAWS are powerful and
not pointed. What the Border terrier men mean by " powerful ", however, does not imply the length and strength of some
of the other breeds of terriers. The NOSE may be either black
or flesh coloured. The EARS are small and curved rather to
the side of the cheek. NECK is of moderate length, slightly
arched, and sloping gracefully into the shoulders. The BACK
is well ribbed up and should not be too long. The CHEST is
narrow, and the SHOULDERS long, sloping and well set back.
The LEGS are true, muscular, and not out at the elbows. The
outer COAT is hard, and there is a good undercoat. The TAIL
is short and well carried, but should not be over the back.
It is not docked. A level MOUTH is required. This Club does
not mention the COLOURS, but the standard of the Border
Terrier Club gives them as red-wheaten, grizzle, or blue-and-
tan. We are reminded by them that " The Border Terrier
is essentially a working terrier, and, being of necessity able
to follow a horse, must combine great activity with gameness."
These dogs grow a naturally short, hard coat that does not
need any trimming for the show bench, and a characteristic
is the moustache that finishes the upper jaw.

I do not know how these terriers came originally, though
the supposition is that they must have been produced very
much from the same strains of terriers peculiar to that part of
the country as gave us the Bedlington and the Dandie. There
is no doubt that they have been bred for many generations in
sporting families resident on the Borders. They have been
made to suit the country in which they work, and their hearts
are bigger than their bodies. Many people declare that a
terrier is incapable of killing a badger singlehanded, but
Titlington Peter, owned by Mrs. Sordy of Titlington, Glanton,
accomplished the feat one day when he was out with the
Percy Hunt, to which he and his kennel-mate Titlington Rap
had been lent by their mistress. At the end of the fight Brock

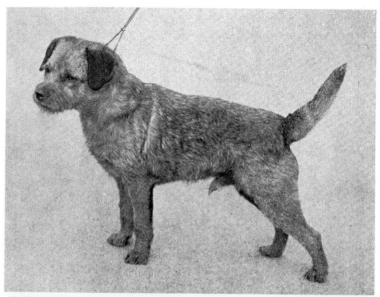

Plates 5—6

THE BORDER TERRIER

Top. CAPTAIN C. R. PAWSON'S KINETON KOFFEY (DOG)
Bottom. CAPTAIN C. R. PAWSON'S KINETON BINKY (BITCH)

was left dead and there remained alive a sorely wounded little warrior much in need of repair. After his jaw had been set and his teeth wired back into their proper position Peter recovered satisfactorily.

There is another story of a bitch named Bess, belonging to Mr. William Barton of New Castleton. When she was running with the Liddesdale hounds, she was put to ground after a fox in a wet moss-hole, and after she had been badly mauled the fox bolted and went to ground again a few miles farther on. Another terrier that was tried having failed to turn him out, Bess was called upon again and she fought him for two hours, eventually making him bolt. Though the bitch needed a good deal of attention, she was about again in a few days ready for work. Naturally in a country of this description, there are many casualties among the terriers, some of which never reappear from the deep moss-holes into which they have penetrated, after their fox. The make of the Border Terriers enables them to enter narrow apertures among the rocks and to jump or climb on to ledges where the fox may have taken refuge. A bigger dog would be useless, and one with legs as short as those of the Sealyham would not be sufficiently active. Digging is seldom possible and it is necessary to have a terrier that can go wherever a fox can.

These sturdy little terriers can run all day with hounds, always being up when they are wanted, and can go out several days a week. A number of English, Scottish and Welsh packs use them outside their native districts, and most Masters who have tried them are satisfied with their work. Their own country is hard going for terriers, much of it being under heather, and for that reason they have to be built on the lines of a small hunter.

Returning for a moment to the origin of the breed, I am reminded that Mr. Jacob Robson, M.F.H., and his father and grandfather before him, had all bred them. This carries us back quite a long way, as Mr. Robson was presented with his portrait in 1926 in recognition of his forty-seven years as a Master. Among the treasures of Mr. James Dodd of Hexham is a letter written to his grandfather, dated 1817, by James Davidson of Hyndlee, who was said to have been the original of Scott's " Dandie Dinmont ". There reference is made to two game terriers, both of which were red. I have seen somewhere that Mr. Davidson had two sorts of terriers, differentiated by their length of leg. The short ones, no doubt, were the progenitors of the Dandie Dinmont, and the others might easily have blossomed into the Border or the Bedlington, outside blood being used to make the latter the racy dog he now is.

THE BULL TERRIER

By COUNT V. C. HOLLENDER

The Bull Terrier is a model of what a dog should be. One of the most perfectly made animals in existence, whose skin fits him like a glove, he is recognized as the gladiator of the canine race. Add to his symmetrical appearance a great, loyal and lovable disposition, absolute reliability, magnificent pluck, high intelligence, and a sense of humour, and here is your model complete in very detail. I do not propose to waste time over his past history or the different blood introduced in order to perfect this fine amateur gentleman. That he belongs to an old breed is undisputed. Sir Walter Scott, who died in 1832, considered that a Bull Terrier was the wisest dog that he had ever owned, and it was a real grief to him when Camp died. Dickens realized his loyalty and noble qualities when he immortalized one, even though it were through the medium of Bill Sykes. I wish it had been possible for me to mention the men and women who in modern times have helped to make the dog what he is, but it would be out of place in this chapter to do more than say that the credit of producing white dogs belongs to the Hinks family, of Birmingham. Up to that time they had been mainly coloured. It is not often that a Bull Terrier has figured in public performances, but it was one of Harry Preston's that kept the Palace Theatre audiences amused for months. In the middle of last century Bull Terriers were looked upon by respectable citizens as disreputable members of canine society, for they were fighting dogs and used for killing rats in a pit, but in later times their admirable qualities have received recognition, and they have been taken up by women exhibitors as successfully as by men. The old pluck endures, and no dog has been of greater service to Englishmen in tropical climates. Innumerable stories could be told of their high courage in tackling wounded big game, and one has been known to have had a fight with a leopard in which the dog did not come off second best, although he was badly mauled. Packs are used in the Far East for hunting wild pig, and, as guards of property and personal protectors, where English folk live among native races, they are unrivalled. As sportsmen and hunters they are all that can be desired. They are strong swimmers, and their retrieving powers have to be seen to be believed. Despite their strong jaws and formidable grip, they are very tender mouthed. In Austria and in many other parts of Europe they act as police dogs.

Let me relate a few anecdotes that I have collected about them. The late Mr. W. J. Pegg repurchased a terror who had only been kept for fighting, but he wanted to use him at stud, though his fighting days were over. He was installed at the bottom of the garden, and no one was allowed to go near him. One day, Pegg, who idolized his grand-daughter, called her from the garden to go to bed. The child made a bee-line for the dog, who was feeding, pursued by the nurse. The child just won, and to Pegg's horror, he being too paralysed to move, she stumbled over the dog, who held the nurse up to let the child do what she pleased. It became a recognized game in the end, and the baby used to make her own terms of surrender by the dog's side. Even Pegg could not go near the child if she were with the dog. Colonel W. M. Douglas bought Charles in Leadenhall Market for £3 and took him to India, where he tackled everything, including bear and jackal. I cannot give a list of all his exploits, but the Colonel concludes in a letter to me about the breed, " He was my first bull terrier, and for pluck, fidelity and gentleness in season I have never met the like of this find in Leadenhall."

Miss Wheatley writes to me of Buck that he was her devoted shadow, and became renowned from Baghdad to Iraq. He killed ten jackal, alone and unaided, and was the greatest sport, the most courageous, yet the gentlest dog, and the most loving and loved companion. She concluded : " May he be waiting for me when I go to the other side." Captain Lugard tells how two tigers from the Kumanon Hills were brought to bay and dispatched before they had time to recover from their surprise at being tackled by a small pack of Bull Terriers. He also relates how a Bull Terrier beat a huge German dog on board a battleship in front of King George. From Harry Preston comes the following : He wished to give a dog during the war to a wounded officer, who, to his dismay, insisted on having a Bull Terrier. " Why a Bull Terrier ? " asked Harry, who was short of them, and knew that the officer was not a doggy man. The explanation was simple. His pal, a flying officer, had gone out one day, never to return. This man's dog used to meet his master on landing, knowing the sound of the engine, which is an accomplishment common to many dogs. He waited hour after hour, and day after day, for the master who never returned, and committed suicide by starving. " So, Harry, my lad, it's a Bull Terrier, or bloody well nothing," said the wounded and much decorated hero, who got one of Harry's very best. May I mention my own dog, not because he was mine, but on account of his merits. He died during the War dragging my tunic out of my quarters to lie on before he passed out. He weighed 70 lb., was human in his intelligence, had a heart as big as his body, was loyal, brave and gentle, a great white gentleman, defeated only by death. He would take messages from one end of London to the other, went on cricket tours with me, and actually found his way to a cricket ground miles away in a strange place. There are four living witnesses to this episode in case it seems to be a very tall exploit. During a bad air raid, when my family descended to the basement, he brought my wife's dressing-gown to her on his own initiative, and I could say much more about his wonderful achievements if space permitted. I would give many years to know that I was going to meet my pal again. My sister's bitch used to take and fetch her children to and from school. Major and Mrs. Warner Abbat gave their favourite dog away after years and he never forgave them for it, but deliberately cut them dead when he met them again. Never give away a mature dog of character who is fond of you. Destroy him first. It would be his choice, and it is the least you can do.

I do not propose entering deeply into the controversy as to the respective merits of the white and the coloured dogs. In recent years, coloured dogs have been revived with a good deal of success. That I like them may be inferred from the fact that I gave Mr. Sievier's Bing Boy his first challenge certificate, Mrs. Ellis's Hunting Blondi his, and Lady Winifred hers. Now for the pros and cons. The coloured, being the oldest, we will take first, though the present modern product is very recent, and from a show point of view streets ahead of anything known in the past. They are less prone to skin disease, and I have yet to know of a deaf one, which is an infirmity to which the whites are very subject. The coloured are better for night work, and are far easier to keep clean. In character there is nothing to choose between them. I have heard it advocated that the coloured are gamer, but this is a pure fallacy. The whites are more typy and as a rule have better-coloured eyes. There was a lot of prejudice against the coloured dogs at the start which still exists in many quarters,

THE BULL TERRIER

Top Left. MISS M. L. GREY'S CH. GALALAW BENEFACTOR (DOG)
Bottom Left. MRS. ADLAM'S CH. RHOMA (BITCH)
Top Right. MR. W. DOCKERILL'S COLOURED BULL TERRIER LADY WINIFRED (BITCH)
Bottom Right. MRS. HONOR McLEOD'S OLD STAFFORDSHIRE BULL TERRIER JIM CRACK (DOG)

and something must be allowed for the contention that it would be hard for the beginner to trace the coloured blood from the pedigrees supplied. Note, the progeny of a coloured dog or bitch are liable to be white. This subject will always be a bone of contention and a problem, but so long as a fine animal of great character is produced, why worry?

Photographs and the show standard explain fairly well what breeders want. As so many fallacies exist where the Bull Terrier is concerned I feel it only right to explain one or two things to prospective purchasers. The Bull Terrier must have a tight skin, that fits him like a glove. His eye should be Oriental-looking and cannot be too black. The so-called red eye is found in guinea-pigs, not in Bull Terriers. He must, above all, have expression and look hard. Complete soundness is essential and he must be active, compact, well-muscled and have good bone and a level mouth. I quite agree with Mr. Croxton Smith, who in writing recently on the breed stated that he always had a great admiration for the well-made bull terrier. After complaining of too many long and slack backs and sleepy expressions, he concluded, " The ideal Bull Terrier looks like a piece of statuary into which life has been infused."

No article would be complete without reference to the genuine Staffordshire pit Bull Terrier. Even if nearly extinct, it is the purest of the lot and nearest to the original type. A few years ago in conjunction with Colonel the Earl of Rothes, we bought some to revive the breed and incidentally to save them from fighting. They have the wonderful advantage of being small, weighing from 16 lb. to 25 lb., yet being men-stoppers at the same time. Their devotion is embarrassing as they insist on accompanying you to your bathroom, and will leave their food, however hungry they may be, in prefer-ence to their owner. The reader will probably wonder why a dog with such virtues is not more popular. The answer is simply that men who keep them are M.F.H.'s and fighting men, who know their value and are terrified lest they should become show bench specimens. The miniature, always game and plucky, suffers from his ugly apple-shaped head. Great credit is due to Mr. Baird, the trainer, and a few others for producing excellent miniatures of the real type and with almost perfect heads. They are dead game. So here is your choice from 10 lb. to 70 lb. You cannot buy affection, but you can buy a Bull Terrier. Use common sense ; exercise and feed him regularly. Play the game by him and you will never regret it.

The Bull Terrier Club's standard of points may be summarized somewhat : The HEAD is oval, almost egg-shaped ; fairly long, but strength must not be sacrificed for length ; of considerable depth ; not too wide or coarse and cheek muscles not prominent. The profile should be almost an arc from occiput to tip of nose, the more down-faced the better ; no stop. FOREHEAD fairly flat and not domed between the ears. FOREFACE longer than the forehead and filled right up to the eyes. MUZZLE should show great strength, and, though tapering, should not be " snipy ". UNDERJAW deep and strong, LIPS tight and clean. EARS small and thin, placed on top of skull fairly close together ; erect, semi-erect, or rose ; eyes well sunken, as nearly black as possible ; small almond-shaped or triangular, nearer the ears than nose. Set closely together, and obliquely placed. NOSE black.

NECK moderately long, tapering from shoulders to head ; very muscular, arched and free from all traces of dewlap or throatiness. SHOULDERS strong and muscular, but without heaviness or loading. Shoulder blades wide, flat, and sloping well back ; no slackness or dip at the withers. CHEST broad, deep from withers to brisket. RIBS well sprung. BACK short, strong and muscular, only slightly arched at loin.

LEGS big-boned but not coarse. FORELEGS moderately high and perfectly straight. ELBOWS should not turn outwards. PASTERNS strong and upright. HINDLEGS straight viewed from behind ; THIGHS very muscular ; HOCKS well let down, and the bone to the heels short and strong. FEET round and compact with toes well arched. TAIL, short, fine, set on low and carried horizontally ; thick where it joins the body and tapering to a fine point.

COAT short, flat, rather harsh to the touch and with a fine gloss ; the SKIN should fit the dog tightly. Pure white coat in the whites. For coloured and Staffordshire : colour (preferably brindle) to predominate.

THE CAIRN TERRIER

By BARONESS BURTON

The Cairn Terrier is probably the oldest authenticated breed of terrier in the British Isles. We read of one of the earlier King James sending a present of some " erth-dogges " to his cousin the King of France. In Mrs. Ross' most interesting book *The Cairn Terrier* she tells the following story :

" In 1600 Donald Gorme Mo'r Macdonald of Sleat and North Uist repudiated his one-eyed wife and sent her back to Dunvegan on a one-eyed horse led by a one-eyed lad and followed by a one-eyed terrier. This infuriated her brother, McLeod of Dunvegan, and started a most terrible clan feud. The Natives were therby so reduced that they fed upon their dogs and cats, but being on neutral ground the terriers of Waternish and Strath escaped."

In 1894 I paid a visit to Waternish, and it was a striking sight to see the Laird of the day, Captain MacDonald, coming down the approach followed by a pack of about 40 of what I had heard called from my earliest youth short-haired Skyes. Captain MacDonald was a very tall and spare old man dressed in home-spun trousers and a black velvet morning coat. The dogs were very level in size and type, what we should call medium-sized Cairns now, and were principally iron-grey in colour. Waternish's first words were " Please don't touch the dogs ; they are too game to be handled." Captain Mac-Donald regularly used his dogs for bolting the otters from the cairns on the sea-shore formed by fallen rocks, and he described how one otter had bolted with 16 terriers holding on to him. Only occasionally were the otters killed by the terriers, which, considering that a dog otter weighs 22 lb., is perhaps not surprising. The terriers bolted the otter, which was then shot.

Another very old strain of Cairns was that of the McLeods of Drynoch, also in Skye. Cairn Terriers were also, and still are, used for bolting foxes, and even to this day are called Fox Terriers in the Western Highlands and Islands, which nomenclature has given rise to mistakes in the Southern mind. There are those who, misled by this appellation, announce that Cairn Terriers were crossed with Fox Terriers.

The first class ever scheduled at a show for Cairn Terriers was at Inverness in 1909 when Mr. Theo. Marples judged, Mrs. MacDonald of Viewfield Portree winning first with Fassie, and Mrs. Alastair Campbell was responsible for the rest of the prizes with McLeod of McLeod, Doran Bhan, and Roy Mohr. By 1911 the Cairn Terrier had so increased in favour that a Club was formed to look after their interests, Mrs. Alastair Campbell being appointed Hon. Secretary and MacDonald of Waternish, President. From that day their popularity has increased by leaps and bounds, and now they more often than not head the list of entries at shows. It is interesting to note that throughout the years Mrs. Alastair Campbell has maintained her position in the front rank of exhibitors. No one will I think contradict the statement that her Ch. Gesto, who was the first Cairn to attain championship status, was THE pillar of the breed.

The Cairn has many qualities to make him the ideal pet for the home. He does not require a lot of exercise, and yet if his master or mistress feels like a long tramp over the moors or fields there is nothing he will enjoy more. They are very good guards, so many of them having a curious sense which enables them to descry or hear the REAL stranger, and therefore they are not perpetually yapping. Cairns are one-man dogs, and their devotion to their master is most touching. They are very intelligent, and it is remarkably difficult to lose a Cairn. He will always find his way home. They are remarkably hardy, as their harsh coat and dense undercoat enable them to defy the cold and wet. The fact that various strains of Cairns were kept by different families accounts for some variation in type, which there undoubtedly still is. The true Cairn is a medium-sized dog, not too short in leg or in back, as it must be borne in mind that length of leg is necessary for the dog to jump onto the big boulders which compose the cairns in which he has to work and one with too short a back cannot turn in an earth.

The GENERAL APPEARANCE should be rugged, with a well-feathered head, the HAIR on which is permitted to be softer than that covering the body. The SKULL should be broad, the EARS small, erect and pointed, and preferably black in colour. The EYE should not be small and black like that of a Scottish Terrier, but of a medium size and dark hazel in colour. A most important point in all Cairns is that they should have eye-lashes, or the expression is ruined. The FORE-FACE should not be too long or strong. The FEET should be round and strong with thick pads. The type to avoid is what is usually described by its admirers as " all a terrier ". This form of dog may be a good terrier, but is always a bad CAIRN Terrier, and is likely to do far more harm than good to the breed as this type of Cairn is always more or less reminiscent of a Scottish Terrier.

The standard of the Cairn Terrier Club describes the GENERAL APPEARANCE as being active, game, hardy and shaggy ; strong, though compactly built. It should stand well forward on forepaws. Strong QUARTERS, deep in RIBS. Very free in movement. COAT hard enough to resist rain. HEAD small, but in proportion to body. A general foxy appearance is the chief characteristic of this working Terrier.

SKULL, broad in proportion ; strong, but not too long or

THE CAIRN TERRIER

Top. THE BARONESS BURTON'S CH. DOCHFOUR EAN (DOG)
Bottom. THE BARONESS BURTON'S CH. DOCHFOUR VUIACH VORCHAD (BITCH)

heavy jaw. A decided indentation between eyes; HAIR should be full on forehead. MUZZLE, powerful, but not heavy. Very strong JAW, with large teeth, which should be neither undershot nor overshot. EYES, set wide apart; medium in size; dark hazel, rather sunk, with shaggy eye-brows. EARS, small, pointed, well-carried and erect, but not too closely set.

TAIL, short, well furnished with hair, but not feathery; carried gaily, but should not turn down towards back. BODY, compact, straight back; well-sprung deep ribs; strong sinews; HINDQUARTERS very strong. BACK medium in length and well coupled.

A sloping SHOULDER and a medium length of leg; good, but not too large, bone. FORELEGS should not be out at elbow, but FOREFEET may be slightly turned out. Forefeet larger than hind. LEGS must be covered with hard hair. PADS should be thick and strong. Thin and ferrety feet are objectionable.

COAT, very important. Must be double-coated, with profuse, hard, but not coarse, outer coat, and undercoat which resembles fur, and is short, soft, and close. Open coats are objectionable. Head should be well furnished. COLOUR, red, sandy, grey, brindled, or nearly black. Dark points, such as ears and muzzle, very typical. In order to keep this breed to the best old working type, any cross with a modern Scottish Terrier will be considered objectionable.

THE DACHSHUND *

By A. CROXTON SMITH

The story of the Dachshund in England may be divided into two phases. When we first took up the breed seriously for show purposes many people regarded them as being of the hound family, possibly being misled by the similarity of the German " hund ", meaning a dog, to " hound ". Consequently, they were bred very largely with heavy, houndy ears, and most of them were too big and cumbersome. We did not realize then that these dogs on the Continent were used below ground as terriers and above ground for beating covert or hunting with their noses. The Germans, in later years, at any rate, favoured the lighter and more active type, and to my mind they are much smarter in appearance than

* We are aware that, strictly speaking, Dachshunds should not be grouped among Terriers, but as much of their work is underground, we have placed them here. Some authorities consider, too, that in more remote times, dogs of this description were forerunners of the short-legged terriers.

the lumbering dogs that I used to know thirty years ago. Thanks to the missionary efforts of Mr. J. F. Sayer, British opinion has been brought into line with the German, but it is only fair to mention that as long ago as 1895 Major Harry Jones, considering that we had taken a wrong turning, imported four dogs from Germany none of which exceeded 17 lb. in weight. They had all won at trials and shows in their own land, but for all that, they were not used to any extent by breeders.

The appearance of the dachshund in this country goes back to the early years of the married life of Queen Victoria, when a number were presented to her and the Prince Consort by Prince Edward of Saxe-Weimar and others. At that time they were used extensively by German and Austrian nobles for sporting purposes and the Prince Consort worked a team in the Windsor Forest coverts for pheasant shooting.

One was exhibited at Birmingham in 1869, and thence onwards the stream of importations was intensified. It is rather strange that the breed should have attracted a good deal of attention in this country before it became the favourite of the German populace. Our Dachshund Club, founded in 1881, is ten years the senior of the German Teckel Klub. It is a pity that we have found no work for them to do, for they are eminently suitable for use in badger digging and other forms of sport. Their extraordinarily powerful jaws and strong teeth enable them to kill rats with celerity.

The late Mr. Walter Winans told me in 1910 that he found them the most suitable dogs for hunting wild boar. He preferred the lighter kind built on the lines of a ferret, some of his weighing not more than about 9 lb. Their size and shape gave them greater mobility in the thick undergrowth of the forests, so that they were as a rule able to avoid the charges of the boar, though occasionally some of them were killed. The bigger English breeds that he tried for this work were too large and consequently suffered many fatalities. For hunting wild boar in the open a cross between English foxhounds and some of the French hounds was liked, but Mr. Winans preferred shooting in the forests where the boar were harboured in dense thickets. He employed a pack that would drive them out until he was able to get in a shot with the rifle. The fir trees apparently that are commonest in these forests are close together, and have their branches less than two feet from the ground, so that beaters cannot force their way through them, but the Dachshunds were ideal.

Mr. Winans once gave me an account of a day's shooting in conjunction with a pack of seven Dachshunds. In an hour he had killed three male boar and the dogs also pulled down without assistance a young male about nine months old after a hunt of two-hours-and-a-half. During that time the line had been crossed by fresh boar but the dogs never showed the least disposition to change. One supposes that in the early days, at least, they were used principally on badger, as " dachs " is the German for that animal. The breed is divided into three varieties, which differ from one another only in coat. The smooth is the most familiar to us, but of recent years the wire-haired variety has made considerable progress and efforts are now being made to popularize the long-haired dogs. Beside these distinctions, the Germans classify them according to weight, heavy dogs being over 15½ lb., the bitches 1 lb. less. Then we have the lightweights, coming between them and the dwarf, the maximum weight of which is 8¾ lb. for dogs and 7¾ lb. for bitches.

The description of the Teckel Klub explains that " the employment of a heavy or light dog depends entirely on local conditions and the kind of hunting for which it is to be used. In North Germany only light dogs are mostly used ; in South Germany, as well as in mountainous districts, the heavy dog ". The following note concerns the temperament of the breed. " Courage to the point of foolhardiness in attack and defence. In play, droll and indefatigable, by nature obstinate and whimsical. With careful training, as faithful, devoted and obedient as any other breed of dogs. All senses well developed. Build and temperament qualify them principally for the hunting of game and vermin underground. Love of hunting, good eyesight and hearing, full voice, small stature, for hunting on the level, well-developed scent for blood-trailing. To answer these qualifications the dachshund must certainly be built according to type ; but to be of practical use, he must also be active, have endurance, and especially be built so as to allow full development of heart and lungs."

In order that a dog may be fit for doing his work comfortably it is important that he should be absolutely sound. The short FORELEGS should fit closely to the ribs and should not be loose at the elbows or turned outwards. The upper part of the legs has an inward inclination and then the lower part and the feet are turned outwards. If they knuckle over at the KNEE it is a sign of weakness, probably arising from a

bad formation and incorrect position of the shoulder. The
CHEST is deep between the legs, forming a keel, thus giving
plenty of room for the vital organs. The dwarf or miniature
dogs are so tiny as to look toyish, but they are said to have
plenty of spirit and to be capable of hunting rabbits or beating
covert. Some German sportsmen use them in shooting black
game, as they bring the birds more slowly past the guns than
do bigger dogs, which alarm them. They are small enough
to enter a rabbit burrow.

German scientists are disposed to classify the Dachshund
and short-legged terriers as members of the basset family.
There is no doubt that dogs of this peculiar form have existed
for several thousands of years. One may be seen on a monu-
ment erected to Thotmes III, who lived about 2,000 years
before the Christian era. The very word, Teckel, which is
synonymous for Dachshund in German may have been derived
from the name of the favourite of King Antifaa II, this dog
having been called Tekal. Professor Pitzinger includes the
basset among the seven principal types from which the many
varieties of dogs have sprung. Incidentally, I was reproved
once for quoting Turberville's reference to the origin of terriers,
my critic pointing out that the original French text translated
by the old Elizabethan contained the word " basset ", which
he thought meant the heavy, short-legged hound that we
know. Personally I was convinced that it meant nothing of
the sort, for our bassets could never go to ground as the old
terriers did. It may have referred to more dachshund-like
dogs from which the short-legged terriers have sprung.

Now to summarize the standard of the Dachshund Club.
In general appearance we have a long and low dog, but
with compact and well-muscled body, neither crippled, cloddy,
nor clumsy. Bold defiant carriage of head and intelligent
expression. The HEAD is long, and appears conical when
seen from above. From a side view it tapers to the point
of the muzzle. Stop not pronounced. SKULL slightly arched
in profile and looking neither too broad nor too narrow.
EYES medium in size, oval, and set obliquely. Dark, except
in the case of chocolates, which may be lighter, and in dapples
one or both wall eyes are permissible. EARS broad, of moderate
length, and well-rounded, relatively well back, high, and
well set on, lying close to the cheek. JAW neither too square
nor snipy, but strong ; LIPS tightly stretched.

NECK, sufficiently long, muscular, clean, and no dewlap,
slightly arched in the nape, running in graceful lines into the

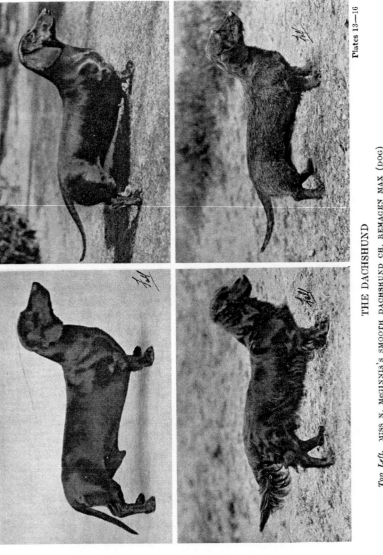

THE DACHSHUND

Top Left. MISS N. McGINNIS'S SMOOTH DACHSHUND CH. REMAGEN MAX (DOG)
Bottom Left. COL. E. J. HARRISON'S LONG-HAIRED DACHSHUND ISOLDA OF DENNA (BITCH)
Top Right. MRS. B. HUGGINS'S SMOOTH DACHSHUND CH. HONEYMOUSE (BITCH)
Bottom Right. MRS. J. F. HARRISON'S WIRE-HAIRED DACHSHUND KINGSWALDON MARTHA (BITCH)

shoulders, carried well up and forward ; SHOULDER-BLADES long, broad, and set on sloping. CHEST very oval, deep, and well sprung ribs towards the loins ; BREAST-BONE prominent.

FORELEGS very short and in proportion to size, strong in bone. Upper arm of equal length with, and at right angles to, shoulder-blade ; elbows lying close to ribs. Lower arm short, slightly inclined inwards and not bending forwards or knuckling over. FEET, large, round and strong.

BODY, long and muscular, the line of back slightly depressed at shoulders and slightly arched over loin, which should be short and strong. Outline of BELLY moderately tucked up.

RUMP round, full, broad, muscles hard and plastic ; HIP-BONE not too short, broad and strongly developed, set moderately sloping. THIGH-BONES strong, of good length and joined to pelvis at right angles. LOWER THIGHS short in comparison with other animals. HOCKS well developed. HIND-FEET smaller in bone and narrower than forefeet. A dog should not appear higher at QUARTERS than at shoulders. STERN set on fairly high, strong and tapering, not too long and not too much curved, nor carried too high.

COAT, short, dense and smooth. Any colour recognized. No white except spot on breast. In red dogs a red nose is permissible, but not desirable. In chocolates and dapples, nose may be brown or flesh-coloured. In dapples large spots of colour are undesirable, and the dog should be evenly dappled all over.

When this standard was framed wire-haired and long-coated dachshunds were not contemplated, so that we have to go to the German Teckel Klub for a description of these varieties. This explains that the body of the wire-haired dogs is similar in all parts to that of the smooths, but at the same time too much stress must not be laid on a very deep CHEST. The COAT is the same length all over except at the muzzle, eyebrows and ears. The MUZZLE grows a beard ; eyebrows are bushy, and the coat is shorter on the ears than on the body, being almost smooth. The general effect should make a wire-haired Dachshund look rather like a smooth when seen at a distance.

In form, colour, size and character, the long haired dachshund resembles the smooth, the only difference being his silky coat, which is soft and gently waved. The legs are feathered at the back, and there is a long flag under the tail. We are reminded that a too plentiful, overloaded coat makes a long-haired dog appear too fat and conceals the type.

THE DANDIE DINMONT TERRIER

By L. IRWIN SCOTT

The origin of this terrier has, in the past, been the subject of much discussion. The weight of evidence of the early history of the breed leads one to think that there was on both sides of the Border—evolved by careful breeding—a short-legged, rough-coated terrier, with pendulous ears, adapted for hunting the otter, fox, etc. Amongst others mentioned in the early records were the family of Allan who kept this breed, and one member of this family, " Piper " Allan, was a noted sportsman and hunter of the otter. Amongst the names of his terriers two favourites are mentioned : Charley, for this dog he was asked to name his own price and replied, " The whole estate would not buy Charley," and for Peachem, a noted otter hunter, the then Lord Ravensworth is said to have offered the life rent of a farm. This offer, also, the " Piper " refused, which goes to show in these early days a good working terrier had in the eyes of his sporting owner a value beyond price. This " Piper " Allan was born in 1704 and died in 1779. The names of several other families are mentioned as keeping these terriers for hunting purposes. In the seventeenth and eighteenth centuries the farmers on the Southern borders had to keep a few terriers to keep down the foxes, and in old parish records on the borders dated 1677 we find 12d. for every fox's head and 6d. for every cub's head was paid.

At a later date we come to a dog called Shem, the property of Francis Somner, bred in 1839 and described as of a bluish-grey colour, with white head, body long and arched at loins, short legs, " a dog of great courage and thoroughly tried at all sorts of vermin ". Mr. Somner purchased a dog called Old Pepper from the grandson of the aforementioned Allan, and Old Pepper was declared to be a descendant of Peachem —Old Pepper was grandsire of Shem. Many of our present-day Dandies trace back to this Shem, and it is interesting to note some of the weights. Shem was 14 lb. Charley, sire of Shem, whose dam came from Hindlee, is described as light grey-and-tan, weight 12 lb., Nettle, a pepper from the kennels of Jas. Davidson, Hindlee, was 11 lb.

In the early days, the breed which had no distinctive name, was chiefly in the hands of travelling tinkers, gipsies, shepherds, etc., and they were highly prized by their owners for their

THE DANDIE DINMONT

Top. THE HON. MRS. S. McDONNELL'S CH. DARENTH SHIAN (DOG)
Bottom. MRS. A. H. SALISBURY'S CH. SALISMORE SPICE (BITCH)

exceeding gameness ; when referred to in the early records they seem to have been used chiefly for hunting the otter, fox and polecat, and many instances of their tenacity are given.

In 1814 Sir Walter Scott published *Guy Mannering,* and the character of Dandie Dinmont, the sporting border farmer, with his numerous pepper and mustard terriers at once took the public fancy, and an immediate and urgent demand for Dandie Dinmont's terriers arose. The public associated Dandie Dinmont with James Davidson of Hindlee, who died in 1820, and since that time the terrier has been known as the Dandie Dinmont Terrier.

The Dandie is a low set terrier with long flexible BODY, well arched over the LOINS. His HEAD is striking, having a broad well-domed skull which gradually tapers towards the MUZZLE, which is powerful ; the TEETH are very strong for a dog of its size, the SKULL is covered with silky white hair—called the topknot. The EYES are full and round, set low and wide apart, of a rich dark hazel colour. These dark expressive eyes, under the silvery white topknot, give the Dandie the quaint look admired by so many. The EARS are pendulous, close hung, and well set back, the fore edge straight, the taper being at the back. They are about 3½ inches long and fine in texture. A houndy type of ear is not desired.

The COAT is distinctive, about 2 inches long, a mixture of soft and hardish hair ; the harder hair coming through the undercoat gives what is termed the pencilled look. The FORELEGS are. short, straight, and very strong, FEET strong and arched with powerful claws ; the TAIL is carried scimitarwise, being of moderate length, strong at the root. There are two COLOURS, pepper and mustard of varying shades. The standard weights are 18 lb. to 24 lb. for dogs, 16 lb. to 22 lb. for bitches. As compared with the weights given of the earlier specimens, the following are the weights of well-known show bench winners of the 1880's : Border Prince, pepper, 23 lb.; Ch. Border King, pepper, 23 lb.; Edenside, mustard, 20 lb.; Champion Linnet, pepper, 20 lb. Within the last few years Dandies have become more popular and are more freely bred and shown than ever before.

The character is one of outstanding determination, and while this is an asset when the terrier is entered it makes the entering a longer job than with some other breeds. The coat is adapted to stand and resist any weather or exposure ; the powerful legs, feet and claws with the flexible body enable the Dandie to dig quickly, and his dour courage and great powers of endurance provide him with an equipment that enables him to hold his own underground.

As far as the Dandie is concerned the programme for entering is much the same as with other breeds of terriers, but it is well to bear in mind and adjust the training to allow for the following characteristics of the breed. They mature slowly, a Dandie at 12 or 14 months being no more forward than say a Fox Terrier at nine, the long arched body does not develop and come to maturity as quickly as the bodies of breeds with shorter backs. At first when taken out hunting they are inclined to be jealous, and unless promptly dealt with, will amongst themselves fight fiercely, especially the bitches. Therefore, in view of this, it is advisable to get the youngsters together sooner than one would otherwise do if one considered only the question of development and maturity. As a rule the bitches are more forward than the dogs, and it is not uncommon for young dogs of from 12 to 18 months to show not the slightest sign of interest in the early training. On this account it is a mistake to draft a Dandie too soon as being unlikely to be a worker, as very often these late starters turn out to be the best in the long run. The early accounts always refer to the Dandie as being largely used to hunt the otter on the border streams, and in many ways he seems specially suitable for this class of work, therefore the few remarks which follow refer chiefly to pre-liminary work with this end in view.

It is a good plan to take the youngsters along the banks of a narrow stream, being careful to select a spot for the first few outings where the banks are low, so that it is easy to clamber out of the water. It is unwise to allow a youngster to get a fright when he finds he cannot pull himself out of the water quickly ; at 8 or 9 months a Dandie is very slack and undeveloped and cannot use himself as freely as other breeds, and this needs emphasizing, and corresponding care in not taking the youngsters to unsuitable water at first. If the stream is narrow and easy of access they will very soon cross and re-cross freely, and if there are a couple of old steady terriers out to feather on any line they may come across, the youngsters will very soon become busy ; now is the time to check any undue signs of jealousy amongst the keener members of the entry. If they are kept at this sort of stream work for short spells it is surprising how quickly they develop a sense of what is required. There need be no hurry to bolt rats at first ; get them handy in picking up and owning a line, and when they get together withdraw the old entered terriers for a bit, and do not re-introduce them till ready to bolt rats, for which a pointed iron prodder will be sufficient—although in the summer evenings the youngsters will doubtless have started many from the dry tussocks of grass edging the stream.

The work can be varied by trying them along a dry ditch when the afternoon sun is on it. A stoat may be started which will provide good sport in and out and liven them up quite a bit. Some people find an easy way to get youngsters keen and clever in water is to take them to a suitable swamp frequented by water hens. These have a strong scent and the youngsters will enjoy the sport and quickly become used to the water, but this plan has its drawbacks, as if the following season the young entry are intended for otter, they will own the scent of water hens and become a nuisance ; therefore it is best to treat water hens as riot right from the start. After a couple of months quiet work one is in a position to discard consistent babblers, also those whose undercoats are not dense enough to resist the water and as a consequence will be tied up with rheumatism later when they have to come out in the early sharp mornings for otter hunting. As a rule Dandies enter at once and go to ground to otter, and if they have been thoroughly disciplined to overcome jealousy, will be found keen and courageous, and, being endowed with plenty of brains, they become very wise and clever at the job. It is now one finds how well the Dandie's coat protects him from cold and wet. There is no shivering on the banks and as the terrier has fully developed out, its capacity for endurance and work is amazing. One or two couples of full-sized Dandies up to 24 lb. are useful when a scrimmage on a ford occurs, their strength and weight tell. If any very dark peppers are in the pack a red band of calico round the neck is a protection. When entered to otter, your terriers will go in to anything else although some at first may not take kindly to the scent of the badger.

The Dandie has a long working life. If at first he develops slowly, he lasts well, is very strong and wonderfully active in spite of his short legs, while his strong skull and powerful jaws and teeth make him an antagonist not to be despised above or below ground. As a rule they work very quietly when entered, attend strictly to the business on hand, and are quick to fall in with the wishes of the person in control, they have

reliable noses as a rule, and their ears do not give any undue
trouble ; in fact, to quote the words used by Dandie Dinmont,
" I had them a' regularly entered, first wi' rottens—then wi'
Stots (or Weasels)—and then wi' the tods and brocks—and
now they fear naething that ever cam wi' a hairy skin on't."

THE FOX TERRIER (SMOOTH)

By N. A. LORAINE

Most of the Fox Terriers of to-day can trace their descent
for some seventy years in direct line, but the first really concentrated effort to produce a terrier on definite lines dates
from the formation of the Fox Terrier Club in 1876, and the
creation of a standard of points for the breed. Of the founders
of the Club I believe that Major Harding Cox is the only one
living. It was he who called a meeting at the house of his
father, Serjeant Cox, in Russell Square. Those present were
Mr. William Allison, afterwards Special Commissioner of the
Sportsman, Rev. C. T. Fisher, Messrs. Abbott, J. A. Doyle,
Gibson, Francis Redmond, Fred Burbidge, so well-known
for his association with Surrey cricket, Theo. Bassett, J. C.
Tinne, and Sydenham Dixon, son of " The Druid " and connected with the *Sportsman* for many years. It was soon afterwards that the standard was drawn up, those who framed it
being hunting men, and so successful was the result of their
labours that it has stood the test of fifty years, and remains
practically unaltered to-day. The sole revision that has been
made relates to the weight. The original standard laid down
that a Fox terrier should not scale over 20 lb. in show condition. The clause now reads : " It matters little what the
weight is to a pound or so, though, roughly speaking, 15 lb.
to 17 lb. for a bitch and 16 lb. to 18 lb. for a dog in show
condition are appropriate weights."

Of the gentlemen named above it will be agreed that Mr.
Redmond did more by his careful breeding to bring the Fox
Terrier to its present high standard than any of them. It
was not long before others joined the Club, and of these the
names of Robert Vicary, M.F.H., and A. H. Clark will always
be remembered. Mr. Redmond put so much stress on the
importance of legs and feet that to-day, if one wants to describe
a dog especially good in these respects, the expression " Redmond legs and feet " covers it. Mr. Vicary seems to have
concentrated more on neck and shoulders, and a good coat.

He always liked a dog with plenty of hair round his throat, his idea being that a terrier required ample protection at that vulnerable point. He would have been horrified at the trimming that takes place to-day.

Besides Mr. A. H. Clark, owner and breeder of the great Ch. Result and Ch. Rachel, mention should be made of others who were closely associated with the fortunes of the breed. There were Mr. J. C. Tinne, the celebrated Oxford oar, and a member of the crew that defeated Harvard in the late 1860's ; Mr. Sidney Castle, who has owned and bred many good ones ; Mr. Desmond O'Connell, breeder of Ch. Oxonian ; and Mr. Frank Reeks, whose " Avons " are world-renowned and the breeder of Avon May, the foundation of much of Mr. Redmond's success. Of a later date we have Mr. Losco Bradley, Master of the Rufford until his death a year or two ago. It is impossible to refer to all but it would not be right to omit Dr. Master, whose well-thought-out breeding operations have met with such pronounced success.

So far I have spoken only of the smooth Fox Terrier and its breeders, but there are also the wires, which are probably the more popular of the two. Nothing more remarkable in the way of the breeder's art can be recorded than in the development of this variety in a comparatively short period. Among the early successful breeders were Mr. Carrick of Carlisle, and Mr. Hayward Field, whose Ch. Briggs and Ch. Miss Miggs were purchased for what was then an almost unheard of figure by the present Lord Lonsdale. The outstanding figure in the making of this variety is the Duchess of New-castle, who is really responsible for the wire-haired Fox Terrier as it exists to-day, for practically every winning terrier traces back to her kennel and to Ch. Cackler of Notts in particular. Cackler of Notts was by Barkby Ben from a daughter of Ch. Tipton Slasher, a hard, game-looking terrier, slightly marked with black on his head and ears. He had a hard, dense coat, and I often think that the really good coats that crop up in the wires are greatly due to Tipton Slasher. The modern craze for whisker no doubt gives the appearance of strength of foreface and length of head, but so much hair on the jaws means a plethora of coat on other parts of the body. To over-come this defect and make the dog presentable trimming has to be resorted to. In fact, nowadays none but an expert can put down a wire fox terrier in show form, but certainly when the job is finished the dog looks smart. Nominally a sporting dog, it seems absurd that the wire Fox Terrier should go through such an elaborate toilet to improve his appearance, but while the demand for so much hair on the face remains the fashion and the foreign market calls for it, so long will the present type of coat prevail.

It is for this reason that the coats of the smooths are more suited for sport. For those who prefer a rough-haired terrier for work there are certain strains with excellent weather-resisting coats and not too much of them, but they will be found among those that are short of this profusion of hair on the face. The modern wire is a game, hard-bitten fellow, and good looking ; as a variety generally better than the smooth in neck and shoulders, also in ears, but not so good in legs and feet. In fact, feet are the weakest point.

There is a common fallacy that the present-day show Fox Terrier is no use for work, but a more erroneous impression could not exist, and survives chiefly among those who have been brought up in the society of the misshapen little beggar figuring under the title of a working terrier, preferably a Jack Russell—whatever that may mean now—or with those who have had no experience of the pedigree animal. The hobby of breeding dogs for show has grown to such dimensions, and is carried on by so many who have no opportunity of working them that, like the town-born child, the produce knows nothing of the country or its ways, but given a chance it is odds on that they will enter into the spirit of their surroundings. It is essential with all sporting dogs that they should be entered properly to the work required of them, as only patience and care will supply you with a reliable working companion. Given this, your shy and nervous puppy may become the best of workers, and more to be depended upon than his over-keen and hot-headed brother. There will be dullards and incapables in all forms of life, and not every puppy bred by the Master of a crack foxhound pack is worthy of entry.

Numbers of the best-known breeders work their terriers. Mr. Redmond, to whom the breed owes so much, was specially keen on the working qualities of his dogs, not only trying them himself but also supplying many Hunts with terriers that earned great reputations in their countries. Mr. Vicary did the same with his Devonshire pack, and Mr. Losco Bradley with the Rufford. Surely it must be in favour of a terrier, as described in the standard of points, that his NECK should be well let into long and sloping shoulders, that his BACK and

LOINS should be strong, his QUARTERS long with muscle well let down into his hocks, that his FRONT should be rather narrow, his LEGS straight, FEET well padded, coat dense and hard, movement sound and free. It is no detriment to the winning hound at Peterborough that he is better looking than the rest. No doubt a Fox Terrier should be built so that he is capable of doing his job, and there is nothing in the standard of points of the Fox Terrier Club to prevent this. It is not the fact of his being well up on the legs—a fox is longer on the leg in proportion to his body than most Fox Terriers—active and capable of galloping that prevents a terrier going to ground, but rather the thick shoulder and wide chest.

After all, it is not the whole duty of a terrier to go to ground, good as some of the ultra short-legged breeds may be for this work. It is annoying to votaries of sport of various kinds to see their terriers, after vainly endeavouring to scramble up a bank, fall helplessly into the ditch. A stout heart no doubt often overcomes physical infirmities, and all honour to the spirit, but it is a sad sight to see the struggle against misfortune. As for brains, endless examples could be given of the intelligence of the show Fox Terrier, but one or two will suffice. Ch. Tan Girl worked with her owner, and was excellent with a gun and as a retriever. Another pedigree bitch accompanied her owner regularly fishing, and as the catch was being landed would enter the water quietly and retrieve it gently to land, where she placed the fish on the bank without a scratch. As long as the fishing went on she entered into the sport with an interest and quietness that were remarkable.

As to the most suitable size for a Fox Terrier, that depends much on the country in which he has to work. Mr. Vicary found in Devonshire that he could use bigger dogs than those that would have been suitable for some countries, and he bred his terriers accordingly. The common idea of a fighting man is a flat nose and a cauliflower ear, and generally a forbidding appearance. Those who saw Peter Jackson, Frank Slavin, Charlie Mitchell, Jerry Driscoll or Carpentier—to name a few—could not fail to be struck with their proportions and almost classical mould, and it is certain that their beautiful balance was a wonderful asset in the ring. It is generally about the best looking horse in the race that wins, and when one thinks of Isinglass, Persimmon, Ard Patrick, Sceptre, Ormonde, Orme, Swinford, Gainsborough, and, a more recent example, Cameronian, it is a reminder that you have the highest courage and capacity with the most perfect shape.

THE FOX TERRIER (WIRE-HAIRED)
By THE DUCHESS OF NEWCASTLE

Every breed of terrier has its adherents, and the great strides made by wire-haired Fox Terriers during the last twenty-five years must be of interest to admirers of this very smart little dog, judging from the long list of annual registrations the most popular in existence. Wires do not boast quite the long descent that their smooth cousins do, as practically every pedigree ends in a smooth tap root, and I believe it was only in the early seventies that they were first exhibited as a distinct variety. Old Jester, Young Jester, Knavesmire Jester, Criterion, Jacks Yarn, Meersbrook Bristles, Meersbrook Nailer, and Meersbrook Ben, all appear very strongly in the old pedigrees. I fear I do not remember any but the last named. There has been a wonderful levelling up since those days, and also since the days of my original Ch. Cackler of Notts, and his seven champion sons Captain and Commodore; both of Notts, Raby Coastguard, Briar Cackler, Sylvan Result, Dusky Cracker and Dusky Cackler, but every winning wire the world over now is descended from Cackler, of which fact I am very justly proud. His sire was Barkby Ben, a double grandson of Meersbrook Bristles, his dam Lady Tipton of Notts, by Ch. Tipton Slasher ex. Partney Prude, by Meersbrook Nailer ex. Ebor Policy, by Criterion ex. the Smooth Ebor Syphon, who in the original Fox Terrier Stud Book traces back eventually to one Lady (E) No. 4824. I think I really stamped my strain by the lucky purchase of Ch. Barkby Ben's litter sister, Barkby Trollop, herself winner of two challenge certificates, as in after years the mating of one of her daughters to Ch. Cackler produced Cobweb dam of Comedian, Crystal and Calyx (dams respectively of Ch. Collarbone and Ch. Corker of Notts.)

I gave a sister of Cobweb to the late Duke of Beaufort, and she proved a real nailer underground.

Comedian was a wonderfully made, but undersized dog, and possessed the very hardest and best wire coat I have ever handled. He played a great rôle as a sire. Amongst his most successful sons were Ch. Chunky of Notts, a little dog with great ribs, perfectly placed shoulders and the best of legs and

THE FOX TERRIER

Top Left. CAPTAIN H. TUDOR CROSTHWAITE'S SMOOTH FOX TERRIER CH. BOWDEN RAKISH (DOG)

Bottom Left. CAPTAIN H. TUDOR CROSTHWAITE'S SMOOTH FOX TERRIER CH. BOWDEN BITTER SWEET (BITCH)

Top Right. THE DUCHESS OF NEWCASTLE'S WIRE-HAIRED FOX TERRIER CH. CHIPPED TIP OF NOTTS (BITCH)

Bottom Right. MR. R. BARLOW'S WIRE-HAIRED FOX TERRIER CH. CRACKLEY STARTLER (DOG) feet. I always feel, though, in his case, that a great deal of credit was due to the smooth cross close up in his dam's pedigree of Mr. Redmond's Ch. Donington, noted for his perfect legs and feet. Chunky did much to correct these points, but I fear they are faults wires still fail in, and they are bad ones for a working dog. Some fifteen male champions come of his line, Wireboy of Paignton being the most famous.

From Ch. Collar of Notts, another son of old Comedian, some 30 male champions descend, the best being Collarbone and Corker of Notts, Barrington Bridegroom, Crackley Sensation, Crackley Sensational, and Gedling Safeguard. I must also not forget the unshown Barrington Fearnought, whose name will always stand out as a sire.

Collar was a very charming, beautifully balanced hound-marked little dog, showing intense quality, and this characteristic has been well carried down to-day.

Another son of Comedian's I cannot forget, although his name does not come down in male line, but I always considered Ch. Common Scamp of Notts the best dog I have bred, a big little one, with absolutely the best legs and feet ever seen on a wire, " they would have done credit to a smooth ". This high praise was given him by Mr. Redmond on awarding him a special for these points. Unfortunately he did not leave much stock behind him, though his blood still appears in some good female lines. Here again was a good smooth cross close up in Scamp's dam.

A fourth son of Comedian's, Olcliffe Captain, was never exhibited. He was a very heavily-marked dog, and like his sire, rather oversized. His blood to-day is the most successful, chiefly through his son Ch. Fountain Crusader, a lovely little dog, who in his time sired five champion dogs, one of them Ch. Talavera Simon, has broken all records, nine champion dogs are standing to his record, and he is still hale and hearty. I believe in this case the strong outcross away from Comedian blood in his dam is a great factor towards his wonderful stud success—he is a medium-sized dog full of terrier style and character. One more champion, descended from Olcliffe Captain must not be forgotten. The American importation, Ch. Beau Brummel of Wildoaks, for he has in his first batch of youngsters produced several champion males already. I have now given a brief summary of the principal sires during this decade, probably many of them from a huntsman's point of view would be called oversized but make and shape must count, and many of these good shouldered well-balanced dogs

would get where a small heavy chested and shouldered little
one couldn't underground. Courage is the real factor, and
I am glad to say that practically every one of the many terriers
I have sent out for work have given good accounts of themselves.

In many cases when a dog gets an undeserved bad name,
it is not that he funks going to ground but it is all the strange
noises and sights above ! (like the cracking of whips, the baying
of hounds)! You must get a dog accustomed to all this
before condemning him the first time of asking. Courage, I
say again, is the real factor, and I hope we never lose it. Just
a word of warning. The craze for long heads and narrow
fronts is doing harm ; we must have back ribs and heart room
to keep constitutions.

During the last two years there has certainly been a slight
down grade, legs and feet badly want attention, inbreeding is
telling its tale, also the continual exportation of the best,
before they have reached their prime. This country has
always been noted as the nursery of the world, and there must
be something radically wrong if American-born dogs can
come and beat the home-bred ones. If we are to keep pre-
eminence we must not allow all the best to leave these shores.

The points of both varieties of Fox Terriers are identical
except for the coat. The standard drawn up by the Fox
Terrier Club explains that the harder and more wiry the
texture of the coat of a wire is, the better. On no account
should a dog look or feel woolly and there should be no silky
hair about the poll or elsewhere. The COAT should not be
too long so as to give a shaggy appearance, but, at the same
time it should show a marked and distinct difference all over
from the smooth species. The points may be summarized to
some extent without destroying their meaning. The SKULL
should be flat and moderately narrow, gradually decreasing
in width to the eyes. Not much STOP should be apparent, but
there should be more dip in the profile than is seen in the case
of a Greyhound. CHEEKS must not be full. EARS should be
V-shaped and small, dropping forward close to the cheek.
Upper and under JAW, strong and muscular ; a fair punishing
strength. There should not be much falling away below the
eyes. The NOSE, towards which the muzzle must gradually
taper, should be black. EYES dark, small and rather deep
set ; as nearly as possible circular in shape and full of fire.
TEETH as nearly as possible level.

NECK clean and muscular without throatiness, of a fair
length and gradually widening to the shoulders. SHOULDERS

long and sloping, well laid back, fine at the points, and clearly cut at the withers. CHEST deep and not broad.

BACK short, straight and strong, with no appearance of slackness. LOINS powerful and very slightly arched. FORE-RIBS moderately arched and back-ribs deep.

HINDQUARTERS strong and muscular, quite free from droop or crouch ; THIGHS long and powerful ; HOCKS near the ground, the dog standing well up on them like a Foxhound, and not straight in the stifle. STERN should be set on rather high and carried gaily, but not over the back or curled. It should be of good strength, anything approaching a " pipe-stopper " tail being especially objectionable.

LEGS viewed from any direction must be straight, showing little or no appearance of an ankle in front. Strong in bone throughout, short and straight to pastern. FORE- and HIND-LEGS should be carried straight forward in travelling, the stifles not turned outwards. ELBOWS should hang per-pendicular to the body, working free of the side. FEET round, compact and not large. Soles hard and tough.

COAT in smooths, straight, flat, smooth, hard, dense and abundant. White should predominate in colour. Red, brindle or liver markings are objectionable ; otherwise this point is of little or no importance.

In GENERAL APPEARANCE the dog must be gay, lively and active ; bone and strength in a small compass are essentials, but this must not be taken to mean that a Fox Terrier should be cloggy or in any way coarse. Speed and endurance must be looked for as well as power, and the symmetry of the Fox-hound taken as a model. The Terrier, like the Hound, must on no account be leggy, nor must he be short in the leg. He should stand like a cleverly-made hunter, covering a lot of ground, yet with a short back. Weight is not a certain criterion of a Terrier's fitness for his work—general shape, size, and contour are the main points : and if a dog can gallop and stay, and follow his fox up a drain, it matters little what his WEIGHT is to a pound or so, though, roughly speaking, 15 lb. to 17 lb. for a bitch, and 16 lb. to 18 lb. for a dog, in show condition, are appropriate weights.

THE IRISH TERRIER

By THE HON. MR. JUSTICE HANNA, K.C.
(*Chairman, Irish Kennel Club*)
and

T. J. WHITE

(*Member of Council of Irish Kennel Club, representing the Working Terrier Association of Ireland*)

There has been much ill-judged guesswork as to the origin, history, and development of the red terrier known as the Irish Terrier. There are, however, some facts quite clear. Dogs played an unusually important part in the life of the ancient Irish people. We have read in the Baerla laws (the very earliest of our Brehon code, recorded in the first centuries of the Christian era) elaborate provisions as to the control of dogs and the responsibility therefor. It is enough for our purpose to indicate that the law recognized the hunting hounds, the shepherds' dogs, and (what we are concerned with) a smaller breed of vermin killers and watch dogs. The hounds were the " dogs of the dignitaries " and the terriers the dogs of the Feini or common people. From the time of the reference to them in the early Laws, they pass almost from sight until more modern days, within which human memory, or " what one old man told another " can operate. Those who have conversed with past generations of sportsmen, have handed down to us a tradition, and a reliable one, that at all times there was in Ireland an indigenous national terrier with an individuality and type of its own, used in its own country for all kinds of sport at earth or river. It had not, in the middle of the last century, reached across the Irish Sea, as it is not mentioned by either Stonehenge or Youatt. Originally the breed varied in colour from dark blue through brindle to wheaten red, and even yet a wheaten pup may be seen in a litter of blues. For some reason, altogether unknown now, the breed split into two types which became more or less earmarked, as to area. The wheaten red terrier was developed in the North into a racier and lighter dog than the blue, though they had in common a fearless and determined gameness. The blue departed less from the original type and remained a powerful and sturdy strain fit for the arduous hunting among the mountains and rocks of the South. The dog we are concerned with was undoubtedly the terrier of the North of Ireland. Though there were some strains of wheaten reds in the counties of Dublin and Wicklow, the main line of geographical cleavage during the first seventy years of the last century was as indicated.

While in the South of Ireland the blues had remained somewhat varying in colour and type, the wheaten red in the North developed in a marked degree, by breeders aiming at the best for sport and appearance, into a more stereotyped dog. He became richer in colour and better balanced in appearance than heretofore. To cut the story short, he made such advances that provision for registering the breed as the Irish Terrier was made by the Kennel Club, and the first show for the breed was held in Dublin in 1873. Mr. J. O'Connor was the first successful exhibitor with his bitch Daisy, the first Irish Terrier entered in the Kennel Club Stud Book.

Once the breed gets on the show bench the progress is easily traced, as type became more firmly settled, and agreement was arrived at, as to disputed points on colour, coat, size, etc. During the first few years after their debut, classes for the breed were confined to Irish shows of importance such as Belfast, Cork, Derry, and Lisburn, as well as Dublin. But by degrees the dare-devils became popular on the English show benches, so much so that in 1879 the Irish Terrier Club was formed, mainly it is true of Irish members, but with some prominent Englishmen (who had become interested in the breed) among their number. This Club continued mainly under Irish control, and with great success, until 1909, when unfortunate differences arose as to policy, with the result that there was a split. Whether or not the breed was waning in popularity compared with some of the new breeds, it began gradually to get on the down-grade as regards numbers, though the quality was well maintained in a few outstanding terriers. Recently the Irish Kennel Club undertook to make special efforts to revive enthusiasm in the breed as being one under their special national protection, and as a result, so far as Irish shows are concerned, the Irish Terrier has again come to its own.

In the early days there were several that stood out and are recognized as providing the basic strains for the breed of later days. The first of notable excellence was Ch. Fly, owned by Mr. N. Morton of Ballymena. She was bred by Mickey Dooey, a famous old-time fancier who believed in the working qualities being developed. To train puppies to water he used to wade into the middle of the river, put the puppy into the water quite gently and then guide it to the bank. Endowed with infinite patience he was famous for bringing out, by his training, the sporting qualities of the working terrier.

The sire of Ch. Fly was Dooey's Sailor, who also sired Ch. Banshee and Dempsey's Jess, the bitch that appeared far back in the pedigree of Ch. Breda Mixer, the outstanding pillar of the breed. Ch. Erin, owned by Mr. W. Graham and bred by Mr. Campbell, near Ballymena, has been called the mother of the breed, and the progeny of her mating with Mr. Waterhouse's Killiney Boy entered into the winning strains for many years. In 1879 she got the first win on the Irish Terrier Club Challenge Trophy, which she eventually won outright. There were also, in the early days, Dr. Carey's Ch. Sting, and Mr. Jameson's Ch. Sport. In those days, that is, the seventies and early eighties, some of the principal Irish exhibitors and breeders were Dr. Carey, his brother Tom Carey, H. Waterhouse, George Jameson, William Graham, E. F. Despard, J. N. R. Pim, J. J. Pim, T. Yarr, R. Ridgway, while the principal English exhibitor at that time was G. Krehl.

Notwithstanding his great popularity as a show dog, or perhaps on account of it, the fine working qualities of the Irish Terrier have been allowed in England, and to a lesser degree, in Ireland, to fall into the background. Before dealing with him as a worker, it would be fitting to say a word by way of description of his principal points.

Of the terrier breeds, the Irish has always been the most racy-looking, with greater range, and the appearance of being built more for speed. At times there has been opposed to this type a more compact and cobby dog, which some prefer, as being more on the lines of other terriers, but the general opinion is that it is not correct, though somewhat attractive, when not clumsy. As to SIZE, in the early days the standard WEIGHT was some pounds less than the present standard of 27 lb. for dogs and 25 lb. for bitches. The older breeders were in favour of the small ones, and some of those mentioned above were not over 22 lb. There will be always extremes of size, following from time to time some fashionable winner, but in the long run the golden mean will prevail. Within the limits of red and wheaten, variety of COLOUR is permitted, so long as the dog is what is called "Whole-coloured", that is, one colour throughout. The reddish wheaten is most characteristic, but bright red and yellow-red are considered sound and not a fault. The texture of the COAT should be hard and wiry, free from soft linty hair or silkiness, but not lying flat or smooth, as this is undesirable. There is a soft, very short close under-

THE IRISH TERRIER

Top. MR. W. S. GREEN'S CH. GALLOPER (DOG)
Bottom. MR. W. S. GREEN'S CH. GRACIOUS (BITCH)

coat of rather oily texture over which the pinwire coat lies with a broken-haired appearance.

Many fanciers, and indeed also the Club standards, lay great stress on the appearance of the head and ears as well as the expression. But it should never be forgotten that a dog has more than a head and ears, and, if he has to work, his body and limbs are of more importance. On the show bench appearance as it attracts the eye counts for much, and many flat-catchers have gone up in the prize list, notwithstanding bad feet and legs, and indifferent body qualities. All terriers should be judged, primarily, from the point of view that they are intended to work at earth or river. The Irish Terrier should have a long flat SKULL, rather narrow between the ears and getting narrower towards the eye. The JAW should be strong and muscular and of good punishing length, but not so long as to be out of proportion to the skull or head or general balance of the dog. The EYE should be dark hazel, small and full of fire and intelligence. The EAR should be small and V-shaped. The HAIR on the face should be the same as on the body, but short, and appearing almost smooth and straight, with a slight beard permissible under the chin. He should be WELL-RIBBED, with level BACK, strong LOINS and good BONE, not too heavy. As a whole the dog must present an active, lively appearance, with lots of substance, but free from clumsiness. Speed, endurance, and power should accompany these qualities. The breed have been called " dare-devils " for their reckless pluck, since, disregarding consequences, they rush for their adversary or quarry. As regards mankind and home life, they have such unbounded affection and great domestication that they make perfect companions.

We claim that the Irish Terrier is sagacious to an outstanding degree, and, if the dog be trained to hunt vermin, this qualification is particularly noticeable. As a ratter, he has no equal in intelligent anticipation, a faculty that is strikingly apparent when he hunts in conjunction with terriers of other breeds. At the age of about ten months he should be brought on ratting expeditions with terriers accustomed to the sport, care being taken to let him join in the kill. Should he show a desire and determination to put paid to the rodents' account, give him every possible evidence of your pleasure, for nothing is more helpful to a dog at any sport than to feel that his owner is co-operating. If a few half-grown rats are provided and released, one at a time, so much the better ;

but when these cannot be got, all that is needed is a few outings
with trained terriers.   If he be hunted with one or two tract-
able Blue Terriers, his co-operation will be found to result in
an increased " bag ", for he watches the movements of his
companions closely ; he knows their indifference to briars and
undergrowth of all kinds, and more often than not, he inter-
cepts the rat while the Blues are tearing through scrub.   The
Irish Terrier is a tip-top water dog, although many believe
him to be inferior to the Blue in this respect, probably because
the red does not take water aimlessly, as the other sometimes
does.   When hunting a rat along the banks of a stream, the
red will take water readily and remain there while necessary.
When our terrier is trained to the ways of rats his anticipation
is uncanny, but to appreciate this faculty more fully, one must
see him worked over rabbits.   He will make the best use of
his nose where rabbits are lying out.   He knows all the likely
patches.   He will beat them methodically ; and, quite frequently, he will stand a set giving ample notice of the presence
of game.   If he knows the district where rabbits are to be
found, he will also know the burrows, and his adroitness in
getting between bunny and the hole very often results in a
comparatively long chase without, however, producing anything more than additional excitement.   No terrier can catch
a rabbit in a short run to a hole ; indeed, our fastest greyhound
will fail to do so under similar circumstances.   The main
object of every sporting terrier should be to nose through scrub
and undergrowth of all kinds, and the Irishman not only does
so, but, by reason of his keenness and agility, his hunting is
particularly attractive.   It is not often that rabbits are found
at any considerable distance from the burrow, but when they
are, our terrier displays great speed and wonderful nosework,
particularly where bunny is forced to seek temporary refuge.
    We have seen an Irish terrier stand " set " to a large heap
of loose stones, three or four yards in diameter, from which a
rabbit was bolted and killed, also the same terrier has stood
steadily to a pheasant, rigid as a gundog, and obedient to
every signal.   We do not hold that every red terrier may be
trained to this degree of perfection.   Many of them are bred
from generations of bench ancestors, whose hunting instinct
has been allowed to lie dormant for so long that it is almost
dead ; but we do hold that, if a dog can be acquired from
some remote part of rural Ireland, a little patient training will
show that, at vermin hunting, he has no superior.   It must
not be supposed that the red is fitted only for the pursuit of

small " game ". His forefather, the wheaten, had no superior over badger or otter, but because of his (the wheaten's) great weight, stronger bone and careful breeding for gameness, he was more adapted to the strenuous work which contact with the badger entails.

A fair proportion of Irish Terriers have inherited the dead-game qualities of the old wheaten, and even after all the years of bench softening many of them are surprisingly good. Two or three years ago we saw one, the property of Mr. Johnston of Dundalk, give a very fine display of gameness in trying to draw a badger from his earth. The terrier was not successful by reason of his weight, being only 26 lb. or 27 lb., but he took all that came to him without flinching and with never a murmur. Some of the Terrier Clubs in Ireland hold trials for terriers during the summer and autumn months, and these trials are divided into two classes. The major or dead game test is for a display of absolutely dead game qualities over badger in natural earth, and the minor, or little test, is for efficiency at rabbit and rat hunting. The slightest sign of hesitation or timidity is sufficient to prevent a terrier being awarded the Major Certificate, and terriers holding it will most certainly " stand their death ", which in Ireland means " will die with the flag flying ". At recent trials held near Waterford, one of the most decisive performances was that of the Irish Terrier, Jumper, who promptly entered the sett, got into immediate contact with a badger, and was absolutely silent till the handler reached him. Of the twenty terriers for trial, some five Blues were as good as Jumper, but the latter was the only representative of the red breed, and he shed glory on it by gaining a certificate. Jumper is aptly named, for he belongs to Mr. Peter O'Connor, Solicitor, Waterford, who for nineteen years held the world's record for the long jump. If the Irish Terrier be bred away from the fashionable bench strains, he will endear himself to all sportsmen as a lovable pal, an intelligent companion, and a thoroughly competent workman ; and while he is the essence of gentleness and amiability, his readiness to keep his end up when trouble brews, leaves no doubt as to his country of origin.

THE KERRY, OR IRISH BLUE TERRIER

By THE HON. MR. JUSTICE HANNA, K.C.

(*Chairman, Irish Kennel Club*)

and

T. J. WHITE

(*Member of Council of Irish Kennel Club, representing the Working Terrier Association of Ireland*)

The Irish Blue Terrier or Kerry Blue as it is called in England and America is the indigenous national terrier of Ireland. In olden times the range of colour was from dark blue to wheaten. From the latter the Red Irish Terrier was developed. The Blue developed on different lines and has an individuality all its own. It went on the registers of the English Kennel Club in the year 1920 and was first shown as a breed at Irish shows in the same year. There have been many thousands registered on the books of the Irish Kennel Club, the first being Mr. Fottrell's Fuamnach

In Ireland the Blue Terrier is, and always has been, pre-eminently a working terrier. He is judged at Irish shows from this point of view and, under the rules of the Irish Kennel Club, Field Trials on rat, river work and rabbit, as well as drawing the badger, are held for the breed, and no Blue Terrier can become a champion unless he has been awarded a certificate as an efficient working terrier at the Field Trials. Drawing the badger is considered the highest test of courage, and for this is awarded the " teastas mór " certificate, while for ordinary sporting work the " teastas beag " is given. These words are Irish for " great test " and " little test."

While extremely domesticated and affectionate, he is inclined to be aggressive towards other dogs, unless restrained, but no breed is more amenable to discipline. His principal mental qualities are a persistent courage, unusual readiness of mind and agility of body and movement. In appearance he is a tousled blue vagabond. On the show bench in Ireland this is, within the limits of reasonable grooming, insisted upon ; but, in England, he is permitted to be shaved and tonsured, until he has quite an artificial and unnatural appearance. There is an unfortunate and irreconcilable difference on this point which prevents free competition between the exhibits in the two countries.

THE KERRY BLUE TERRIER

Top. COLONEL JOE McLAUGHLIN'S INT. CH. CRANA CONUNDRUM (DOG)
Bottom. THE MISSES H. K. & H. HENRY'S CH. BEN-EDAR BLITHESOME (BITCH)

The three outstanding features of the Blue are his build, his coat and his colour. He is a sturdily-built dog between 35 lb. and 40 lb. WEIGHT, better 35 lb. than 40 lb. One does not look for the extremely narrow SKULLS or fronts, nor for the long forefaces that are so popular in show specimens of some other terrier breeds. He should have good spring of RIBS, and HINDQUARTERS of marked strength and muscle, and should be well coupled. His MOVEMENT is light and quick, but with none of the high stepping gait. His EYE should be dark and well set but not too small, nor with the large soft expression of the spaniel. Light eyes and soft expression are faults.

The Blue is a one-coated dog. He has no UNDER-COAT. It should be very full all over the body and of a soft silky texture, lying in almost ragged broken waves with some tendency to curl. But ringlets or too pronounced curl is to be avoided as much as the straight coat. The former is from some ancient Irish water spaniel blood, and the latter from hard-coated terrier blood. The COLOUR should be dark steel blue, from which the dog gets his name, but any blue from dark to light grey blue is right. In adult dogs black or whitish-grey are wrong. All-browns, mottles or particolours are also wrong. For his sporting work he must have a deep strong JAW, with level MOUTH of perfect TEETH, overshot teeth are a bad fault. The FEET should have full round pads, but not cat feet, being round, well shaped, with black nails. A flat thin foot is a fault. The bone should be in keeping with the true sturdy appearance of the dog.

Having a good typical terrier in our mind we can explain the methods of training for work. When man and dog join forces in pursuit of vermin, each helps the other to acquire a knowledge of the ways and haunts of vermin, and this co-operation is a joy to the dog and an incentive to him to use his instincts to the full. The training of a sporting terrier should be undertaken by a person who has some knowledge of the adaptability of the dog for the work in view.

In dealing with the Irish Blue Terrier or " Kerry ", it might be well to state at the outset that the dog has no equal as an all-rounder. He combines excellent nosework with a partiality for water where rats are the quest, and, if properly bred, he is absolutely dead game to badger and otter. He is much too robust for fox, which he will kill as quickly as he will a rat. Let us take a nine-months old puppy and give him a course of rat and rabbit training, to be followed

by an introduction to badger when he is almost mature. He
has had complete freedom during his puppyhood, and will
play with any terrier that may happen along. We mention
this to induce owners to give their terriers as much freedom
as possible, for Blues that are put under restraint are apt to
expend surplus energy in fighting.

Highly strung terriers are sure to come to grips at some
time or other, and when the Blue fights he holds. He should
not be beaten whilst fighting, or have cold water thrown
on him as an inducement to cease—this only aggravates the
trouble. Experience will show that as a rule only one of
the contestants will have a hold. Two persons must co-
operate in the parting of them ; one should hold the loose
dog, that is the one that has not got a grip, and keep all
feet off the ground, the other should lift the dog with the
grip and place the loins between his knees, catch him by the
neck, close to occiput, with left hand, and with the right
bring to bear what pressure he is capable of on the windpipe.
Ten or twelve seconds should suffice to break any hold, but
while this is being done care must be taken that the other
dog, or the badger as the case may be, does not have a chance
to catch the hand.

Proceed to give our puppy a lesson in ratting. Rats are
to be found along the banks of streams or canals, particularly
in the vicinity of towns and where rubbish has been deposited.
As a preliminary we obtain a couple of rats, caught in a cage
trap, and release one in sight of the dog. He pounces upon
it and kills with determination, at which we pat him to show
our approval. We release the second one in a field where
there is about three inches of grass, but not in sight of the
dog. After the lapse of half a minute the terrier is released
and directed to the spot where the rat was allowed to escape.
He picks up the scent at once, and may run the line truly
or lose it momentarily, in which case he returns to his base
and again takes up the line, this time more slowly. He must
not be urged to go ahead, we keep him to the line by direction
if we know it, but otherwise he is left entirely to his own
resources. He soon finds, and kills again with vigour, for
which we show our pleasure. We now look for a light steel
bar about four feet long, one end being pointed, and if there
be no blacksmith in our locality the tooth of a hay rake will
serve our purpose. As it is late Spring or early Summer
(the best time of year for such work) we wander along the
banks of a stream, and since our terrier has been in water

many times he takes to it quite naturally. We make a show of looking into all the likely cover we meet with, and our dog is most assiduous in his quest. He becomes very excited, dashes into some overhanging briars and a rat takes to the water unseen by him. We have our eyes open however, and we direct the terrier, who " marks down " the rat.

Our steel bar is of great use now ; it helps us to follow the course of the hole and we find that a spade is needed. We borrow one, and in a little while we force the rat to water, which it takes almost under the dog's nose. Excitement is high, we restrain ourselves with difficulty from throwing stones to direct the terrier. We point to where we see the rat come to the surface and the dog sights it also. Another dive, and while the terrier is treading water the rat reappears under some bushes through which it tries to escape. Our dog tears after it, and briars and brambles offer no resistance to his impetuous ardour. The rat takes the water again but cannot remain under for more than a few seconds, and is killed and retrieved.

Two or three such afternoons and a day with a friend who owns a really good ratter works wonders for our dog, who does most of his hunting from the water. He finds that our friend's terrier hunts the bank very well and that nearly every rat takes to the water.

In the course of a couple of months our tyro has become an expert at rats, and we decide that we shall give him an opportunity to get acquainted with rabbits. We procure a couple of live rabbits through a man who keeps ferrets (they can always be got for a couple of shillings each). We release one in a field where there is good cover, and when it has taken the nearest, as it usually does, we put our Blue on the trail. He is a bit slow at first, but picks up the scent, and as he gets accustomed to it, works his way to the cover. We do not disturb the rabbit, it is better to let the dog do that, and as he gets close to his game, the latter bolts to a fence in full view. We see to it that somebody is on the other side but we give our terrier no further assistance than an occasional direction by hand. It is odds on the dog, for rabbits are particularly foolish when taken from their own haunts. Two or three rabbits released in heavy cover will give our Blue a perfect nose for them, he will set like a gundog and go through heavy scrub and thorn with the utmost boldness.

Each outing, whether over rats or rabbits, has a steadying effect on the dog, and as he approaches fifteen or sixteen

months of age we decide to put him to the one sport for which
he is pre-eminently suited both in temperament and physique,
namely the drawing of a badger from the natural earth.
We are informed that a not-too-heavy Sett is within a dozen
miles of us.

We require two really good underground terriers, or
Sounders, as they are called in Ireland, four or five hefty
diggers, one of whom should have a knowledge of earths,
and the following implements, viz. 3 spades, 3 shovels, 2 picks,
1 mattock, 1 slasher or bilhook, 1 triangular hoe and 1 torch.
The important points to note are, let the Sounder have at
least a quarter of an hour to drive the badger to his last line
of defence, and when satisfied that he has reached it, cut a
trench at least three feet wide and sufficiently long to intersect
all pipes connecting the inhabited portion of the Sett (the
badger will rarely lie near the centre of it) from the main
part of the earth. This to insure that the badger does not
charge the Sounder and undo all the work by getting back
to the labyrinth of pipes in the heavy part of the Sett. Our
earth specialist advises us that all pipes are now cut through,
that he has found the occupied one, and that he can induce
the Sounder to desist when we are ready to call for him.
Now for the hoe and torch ; we are seven or eight feet from
the Sounder and we inspect the pipe. It will need to be
enlarged to about 6½ inches in diameter, and when this is
done the little terrier is induced to come out, for an impetuous
Blue excited by the strong, and to him, unusual scent, will
catch the terrier as readily as he will the badger, until he has
had sufficient experience to discriminate. The Blue goes in
with dash and establishes contact with the badger. There
should be no sound, beyond the scuffle of pull and resistance,
and the torch will throw light on the situation. The man
at the pipemouth must know the probable angle of the bend
in which badger and terrier are engaged, and as it will be
physically impossible for the dog to draw the badger round
that bend, the corner should be broken with the hoe, and
the terrier given as much room as possible. Provided he has
been silent in his work and has taken what punishment came
his way without a murmur, he is drawn as soon as he can be
reached, and he will most certainly be attached to the badger.
He has done the right thing so far ; we do not let anything
in the nature of a fight take place in the trench. We take
the badger by the tail and see that his mouth is engaged
while my friend chokes off the terrier, as already explained.

In Ireland if a Blue does not go to badger first time of asking he is given the benefit of the doubt ; the hole mouth is broken till the terrier may be put in actual contact, and if he shows the white feather he is presented to a political opponent.

The standard of the Kerry Blue Terrier Club of England requires that the HEIGHT at shoulder of dogs should be 18 inches; bitches slightly less ; WEIGHT, dogs 33 lb. to 35 lb. ; bitches, 30 lb. to 33 lb. HEAD long and strong, SKULL flat, very slight stop, JAWS strong and deep, nearly level with cheeks, MOUTH even, strong, and TEETH level, NOSE black. EARS not too heavy, V-shaped and carried close to sides of the head or over the eyes. EYES black or dark brown, showing fire and intelligence.

NECK muscular and moderately long. SHOULDERS well sloped to back. CHEST muscular and deep, neither full nor too wide. BACK strong and straight. Medium length, well coupled. LOINS broad and powerful. RIBS fairly well sprung, deep rather than round. HINDQUARTERS strong and muscular, showing good development. THIGHS powerful. HOCKS strong and near to the ground. FEET strong and fairly round. TOE-NAILS black ; PADS clear of cracks. FORELEGS straight, plenty of bone and muscle ; ELBOWS working clear of sides. TAIL carried gaily, but not curled over back.

COLOUR, any shade of blue from light to dark ; slight tan allowable up to age of eighteen months, after which tan markings to constitute a disqualification. COAT soft to touch ; weather resisting. Head and feet should be clear, body full-coated, but tidy. In GENERAL APPEARANCE the dog is active, hardy and wiry, with plenty of substance, indicating strength without clumsiness. Must show gameness and intelligence.

THE LAKELAND TERRIER

By R. CLAPHAM

The English Lake District has always been famous for its working terriers, but until recent years there has never been a standard type. Now, however, a few breeders have established such a type under the title of Lakeland Terrier.

For the most part the terriers used by the fell Hunts in Lakeland are cross-bred, with Bedlington, Border, etc., blood in their veins. They have never been bred for show purposes, but solely for work against hill foxes. That they do their

work well, anyone can testify who has had a season or two
with the fell packs.

The establishment of a show type of terrier may or may
not benefit the breed, but in my experience show terriers are
apt to get much too far apart from the working sort, especially
as regards size.

The work that a Lakeland Terrier has to do is very different
from that of a terrier in an ordinary hunting country where
foxes have to be bolted from drains and other comparatively
easy places. On the fells of the Lake District the foxes resort
to rock earths, locally known as " borrans ", some of which
are of large extent and great depth. These rock earths are
composed of masses of piled-up boulders, debris for the most
part, which at some time or other has fallen from the crags
above. Such places may be dry or wet according to their
situation. There are, too, certain disused quarries on the
fells in the ancient rubbish heaps of which the foxes also
take refuge. Some of these rubbish heaps are worse places
to bolt a fox from than the ordinary rock earths. The Fell
Foxhound packs which are followed on foot, hunt for sport
as well as to keep down the hill foxes which so often play
havoc with the farmers' lambs in spring. If a hunted fox
gets to ground and bolts, well and good, if not he has to
battle for his life against the terriers. Usually he succumbs
during some period of the encounter, but on occasion he may
hold the upper position on a ledge and mete out punishment
to his attackers, while on a few occasions the terriers may
fail to get at him or even find him at all. A fresh fox will
often bolt quickly from an earth, whereas one that has been
hard run will generally fight to the death underground rather
than trust himself in the open.

In addition to facing foxes, a Lakeland Terrier has to
follow the huntsman over all sorts of rough mountainous
going with perhaps some inches of snow on the ground.
Climatic conditions are often very severe indeed on the high
tops and unless a terrier is a real hard sort with a good coat,
he may have to be picked up and carried or as has happened
before now, he may die from exposure. There is no mounted
terrier-man to carry him in a comfortable bag. He has to
rely entirely on his own legs, and often submit to being hauled
about by another terrier to which he is coupled. His life is
therefore not altogether a bed of roses.

Amidst the subterranean ramifications of the rock earths a
terrier is faced with all kinds of obstacles. He may have to

THE LAKELAND TERRIER

Top. LADY ELIZABETH HOWARD'S FINN (DOG)
Bottom. MRS. GRAHAM SPENCE'S EGTON LADY OF THE LAKE (BITCH)

slip down a steeply inclined place, and scramble up another. There may perhaps be a narrow perpendicular crevice to squeeze through, or an equally tight horizontal crack to be negotiated. A fox can squeeze through a very tight place indeed, and if he then turns to give battle he sometimes has the terrier at his mercy. Again a terrier may easily get far down into an earth, and then fail to find a feasible way out. Many a good terrier has been lost in some of the big borrans, while others have been rescued by willing workers after being incarcerated for several days and nights. In order to do the work required of him both above and below ground, a terrier for use on the fells should conform more or less to the following specification : WEIGHT 15 lb. to 16 lb., COAT, thick and wet-resisting ; CHEST narrow but leaving sufficient room for free action of heart and lungs, LEGS sufficiently long to enable the dog to travel above ground easily, TEETH level, and JAWS powerful but not too long ; EARS preferably small and dropped close to the head. The most important points are narrow chest, good coat, and sufficient length of leg. A narrow-chested terrier, even if a bit on the leg, can go where a broad-chested, short-legged dog would fail. Length of leg enables a terrier to cover many miles of country during a long day and enables it to jump up places underground where a short-legged one would be handicapped. A dense, hard coat resists snow, rain, and cold. In many Lakeland Terriers there is a good deal of Bedlington blood. The latter is often accompanied by a fineness and silkiness of coat that forms a poor protection from the weather. In the usual type of show terrier, the FORELEGS and FEET are overdeveloped, by which I mean that the legs are too straight, and the feet too round and cramped. The fox is a wonderful climber and negotiator of rough ground, because it is back-at-the-knee, with elongated or hare-feet, and well developed dew-claws. Given a fair length of pastern in an oblique direction, plus a hare-foot and efficient dew-claws, a terrier can pull himself up places where another with a round foot, short, straight pastern, and no dew-claw would fail. The show terrier may do well enough for working drains and simple places, but big rock earths are not simple, thus the show type is not the most efficient for use on the fells. In addition to the points of conformation above mentioned a terrier should throw his tongue well when he gets near his fox so as to let those above ground know what is going on. Lakeland Terriers come in almost all COLOURS, grizzly or black-and-tan being common.

In the case of a working terrier, courage is of course indispensable. A terrier may have ideal shape and make, but if he has not the guts to go up to his fox he is not worth his keep. It is wonderful how a real good one that is perhaps handicapped by his size will eventually get there somehow, solely because he is determined to come to close quarters with his quarry. A faint heart is no use to a terrier, a horse, or a man.

On the fells the hill foxes sometimes turn the scales at 20 lb. in the case of extra heavy specimens. A terrier that has to deal with such a fox amongst the labyrinths of a rock earth, has his work cut out. Once he gets right at his fox the latter has to bolt or die, for a courageous terrier is a match for the biggest fox living. It is when the fox is up on a ledge, or snapping at the terrier through a narrow crevice that the dog gets the worst of it. In a big rock earth more than one terrier is usually let go, and they help each other.

When it comes to entering a young terrier, it is well to choose an easy place if possible, and let the young one work in conjunction with an older dog that knows his job. Lakeland Terriers are for the most part demons at fox or otter, but inexperienced with badger. A game terrier that will go straight up to a fox or otter, is likely to get unmercifully punished if he tries the same tactics with a badger, and it is therefore unfair to use him for that quarry if experienced badger terriers are available to take his place.

THE SCOTTISH TERRIER

By W. L. M^CCANDLISH

It may be said of the Scottish Terrier that he is an engineer's job, a job designed to meet peculiar needs ; yet it would be an exaggeration to profess that he was produced purposely to obtain certain working requirements. Before the days of shows, there may have been an occasional owner who bred a family of terriers to a type of his own device, but there can be no doubt that the vast majority of the indigenous dogs of the highlands of Scotland were not bred, they happened. Nevertheless he is an engineer's job, and through the centuries he developed to suit the needs of the locality in which he lived. It must be admitted that this development resulted in a variety of patterns, and, with these varieties before us, it is for us to decide which is the best construction

for the work that has to be done, because there must be one
form of construction superior to all others could we but tell it.
The trouble is that, in breeding dogs for work, we choose as
our material the dogs we know to work best, we depend on
individual prowess. In the individual the heart is of more
importance than the make and shape, and we may get a
race of dogs who work extraordinarily well, notwithstanding
grave defects in construction. The fear is that, in time, the
great heartedness depreciates, and we are left with a type of
dog severely handicapped by its wrong construction. Physical
form is of importance, and the ideal dog is the one with the
stoutest heart in the soundest body. If, in the pursuit of the
stout heart, we lose the ideal formation we move towards
ultimate deterioration, just as surely as when, in pursuit of
the ideal formation, we lose the stout heart. We may be
unable to describe the stout heart, but we may, within limits,
determine the ideal physical formation.

The first essential is a low centre of gravity. The dog
must be able to retain its balance along rocky ledges, to
scramble its way among rocks and stones where no dog with
a high centre of gravity could possibly go. The shortness of
the Scottish Terrier's legs is not for underground work, but
for getting about above ground. The need is not for a short
leg but for a low hung body. In fact, the agility needed for
getting over broken ground demands length of leg, and the
mechanical problem solved in a Scottish Terrier, is getting
the agility of length of leg with the balance of a low centre
of gravity. A dog's FOREHAND consists of shoulder-blades,
humerus and foreleg, and its quarters consist of pelvis, upper
thigh, lower thigh and hindleg. It will be apparent that, if the
shoulder-blade is placed vertically above a vertical humerus on
a vertical foreleg, the top of the shoulder-blade will be much
higher from the ground than if the shoulder-blade is placed
upon a humerus at forty-five degrees and if the humerus
is placed horizontally with one end on top of the vertical
foreleg. In the same way the top of the pelvis will be much
higher from the ground if it and both thighs are placed
vertically over the leg, than if each is placed diagonally and at
right-angles to each other. The tops of the shoulder-blade
and of the pelvis are connected by the spine, and, consequently, it is easily perceived that if a dog's body is carried
on the vertically placed structure it is very much higher from
the ground than if it is placed on the structure where the
bones are at angles the one to the other. This description

is of course an exaggeration, but it is on this principle we get an animal low to ground and yet without much loss of agility through shortness of leg. Such loss as there is, through shortening the bone and therefore shortening each muscle, has to be made up for by an increase in the mass of muscle. Guided by this knowledge we can describe the build of a Scottish Terrier. The SHOULDER must be long, the HUMERUS, also, relatively long and at an acute angle to the shoulder. This leads to a prominent brisket and the appearance of much of the body as in front of the foreleg. In HINDQUARTERS the dog must have a well-bent stifle, for that is the sign of bones correctly angulated, and the bend at the stifle is the hall-mark of efficient construction of any terrier whose gravity has to be set low. Moreover, this construction enables the animal to have much greater mass of muscle than when the thighs are more vertical. Length of muscle is strength, length of muscle depends on length of bone. By placing the bones at acute angles to each other, we get a lowered centre of gravity without loss of length of bone. The low set body has a further advantage. What may be called the business end of a terrier is its mouth. The whole construction of a battleship is centred round the turrets; everything else exists for efficient use of the guns in the turrets. The jaws are to a terrier as the turrets to a battleship. The whole construction of a terrier is to bring the JAWS into action in the right place, at the right time and in the most efficient and economical manner.

To get the jaw to the scene of action we depend on the construction of body, legs and feet. In action the base on which the machine, otherwise the jaw, works is the body. No machine works well on an unsteady base. We cannot have as solid a foundation as that of immobile machinery, but a dog hung low to ground, with a concentrated body heavy for the size, is much more firm than a lightly built body on long legs. Once in action every muscle in the dog's body comes into use, the whole machinery of the ship is in being, serving the needs of the weapon of offence.

On a correctly constructed framework of forehand and hind-quarters there is built a body of great power in a small compass. The SHOULDERS must lie flat since we want fair width of CHEST with no heaviness to impede action underground; RIBS must be well sprung and carried right back, and deep for heart room; the loin very muscular and goodly buttocks and hams. Power and sturdiness, quick in action but hard to shift with big and strong quarters to act as the base of the

THE SCOTTISH TERRIER

Top. MR. R. CHAPMAN'S CH. HEATHER NECESSITY (DOG)
Bottom. MISS WIJK'S BRILLIANT OF DOCKEN (BITCH)

offensive machinery. Controversy there is on what is called length of body, but words like long and short have no meaning in themselves; to have a meaning they must be relative to something else. For stamina we seek a closely coupled animal when, with it, we get liberty of movement. The SHORT LEGS make the body look longer than it is, yet the short legs demand a slightly longer loin than in a longer legged terrier. If, instead of thinking about length, we get the fulfilment of the two ideas of activity and strength there cannot be much wrong with the body. Another misconception that arises through the wrong application of words, is when it is said a Scottish Terrier should be low to the ground and it is assumed from this that the legs should be short. If we keep in mind the simile of an engineer's job, we shall know there is no merit in short legs, they are forced upon us for a reason other than their length, and should be no shorter than will serve that purpose. The FEET should be of fair size and very thickly padded. The body should be covered with short fur for warmth and an outer coat of hard hair as a protection and to resist weather.

The HEAD is all-important. We look to it for the expression of a dog's character ; in the skull lies the brain, the controlling centre, and in the muzzle is the feature of every terrier's existence. The jaws of a pair of pliers have no power, they must have enough strength to resist power applied through them, but the power is applied behind the fulcrum. There must be a certain amount of strength in a dog's jaw, but to speak of a powerful jaw is a misnomer. The power is in the muscles attaching the jaws to the skull, and dispute arises as to the shape of skull which best provides pressure between the jaws. Some say it should be short and broad, others that it should be long and relatively narrow. As mentioned earlier, these adjectives have no significance in themselves, and a long skull relatively narrow may be actually broader than a short thick skull, especially if the eye is further deceived when the MUZZLES of the two types of head are also relatively long and relatively short. If, within reason, length adds strength to a muscle, then length of skull permits of a longer muscle and provides the stronger grip of jaw. There may be little advantage in a long jaw, and a short jaw may give the quicker bite, but a certain length of jaw balances good length of skull if the jaw is an engineer's job. For these reasons the perfect head of a Scottish Terrier is one with a skull of considerable length giving the appearance of being relatively narrow with no cheekiness, and the muscles lying close to the side of the head ; a muzzle of fair length tapering towards the nose, which should be of good size and protrude over the mouth, the teeth large and the incisor part of the upper front teeth overlapping the lower teeth, and the gallery of the upper teeth resting on the lower. With such a head there is plenty of room in the skull for brains and, if a dog has no sense, it will not be caused by lack of space.

What I have written may not be a description of the work a Scottish Terrier should do, but it gives a description of the ideal dog to do the business of a highland terrier, the extermination of tod, brock and foumart, and, if a breeder succeeds in breeding such a dog, it will win prizes on the show bench as a Scottish Terrier. It can also, in lighter moments, hunt rabbits along a brae face covered with patches of juniper, bracken or bramble, and, should it break cover at the scut of the quarry, by the time the rabbit has gone ten yards, the rabbit's extra pace in the open will make it a safe shot for the gun.

THE SEALYHAM TERRIER

By FRED W. LEWIS

There is very little resemblance between the original Sealyham Terrier and the show type Sealyham of to-day. The former was intended solely for sporting purposes and was a small active little animal rarely weighing more than 16 lb., and not infrequently 14 lb:, which was the weight most favoured by the founder of the breed, the late Capt. Edwardes, of Sealyham, Pembrokeshire, whence the dog derived its name. The original Sealyham was in no sense a low, thickset animal like the present-day prize-winners ; indeed, had he been made after this fashion it will be obvious to all sporting readers that as an adjunct to the founder's pack of otter hounds the Sealyham would have been perfectly valueless. Therefore, the introduction of the Sealyham to the show ring with the consequent change in type may be said to have ruined the breed as a terrier for all round sport. Of course, the modern type of dog is still a very useful animal for ratting and rabbiting, while those of the smaller variety are quite suitable for badger digging and even for bolting the otter and fox.

The question is often asked : how does the modern Sealyham

THE SEALYHAM TERRIER

Top. MRS. C. CHARTERS'S SWELL FELLA (DOG)
Bottom. MRS. T. A. M. HILL'S CH. REDLANDS RISKY (BITCH)

compare with its original ancestors in the matter of endurance and pluck? There is no doubt in my mind that in this respect as a breed it has greatly degenerated, and the reason is not far to seek. I remember when the chief recommendation of a stud dog was its usefulness underground and its reputation for transmitting this feature to its progeny. But the provision of classes at shows with the allocation of challenge certificates by the Kennel Club entirely regardless of whether the competing dogs were hard-bitten or not, turned the attention of breeders away from the sporting aspect of the matter and centred their interest wholly on the reputation of stud dogs which had acquired a good name as a sire of prize-winners. Thus matters went on so that to-day the character of a stud dog is assessed entirely on its potential value as a sire of winners at shows. This change-over has, however, rendered the Sealyham more popular than ever. The reason for this no doubt exists in the fact that the general public have had opportunities of making its acquaintance at shows, which previously were restricted to the comparatively few who used the breed for work.

The Show Sealyham is undoubtedly a very handsome, attractive animal, and when one compares the prize-winning specimens of to-day with those which were first benched at the Crystal Palace Show in 1910 the improvement which has been effected is truly astonishing. Many authorities argue that the craze for a powerful, and what is termed a punishing jaw has been carried to excess, and, although this is to some extent true, there is now a decided tendency amongst most judges to favour a type free from very pronounced exaggerated features. Hence breeders are striving to produce a well-balanced terrier if possible of a WEIGHT rather under than over 20 lb. for dogs, and 18 lb. for bitches.

The JAW of the Sealyham should be square and deep rather than long as in the Fox Terrier, while the EARS are distinctly larger, are slightly rounded at the tips, and should be carried at the side of the cheek. The SKULL is supposed to be slightly domed, and should incline to wideness between the ears. A reachy NECK which is likewise strong and muscular ought to be well set on sloping shoulders. Unlike the Fox Terrier, the CHEST must be broad and deep, and well let down between the shoulders. The BODY is of medium length, the idea being to afford flexibility of movement when working an earth. The LEGS and COAT are points of high importance. The former must be short and as straight as possible and the coat

F

long, hard, and wiry.   In the show ring to-day these standard points are ignored as trimming is carried to such lengths and performed with such a degree of skill that it is very difficult, especially for an amateur, to detect the difference between a good and bad jacket.   In GENERAL APPEARANCE the Sealyham ought to be a jaunty, sporting little gentleman, either all white or with head markings.   Body marks are now very rarely seen, and if they extend to beyond a patch at root of tail are viewed with disfavour by most judges.

The Sealyham as a rule is amenable to most forms of sport, but ratting and rabbiting are the principal vocations to which its sporting proclivities are applied.   At the age of six months most Sealyhams will kill rats, but it is inadvisable to give a puppy a large rat as a beginning.   As is well known a big rat can inflict heavy punishment on an inexperienced youngster, and for this reason a few small rats should be provided for the first lessons.   There are plenty of Sealyhams which will kill rats given to them readily enough but which display little aptitude for hunting.   To develop a taste for hunting I have found it an excellent plan when a puppy has acquired a keenness for killing rats to place a bundle of straw in a loose box, garage, or similar building making sure beforehand that any spaces through which the rats might make their escape have been previously stopped up.   Then turn down as many rats as are available, and when they have concealed themselves in the straw let the puppies in and encourage them to search the bedding.   Their scenting powers will quickly enable them to detect the presence of the rats, and as it will require quite a bit of nosing in the straw to get to grips with the quarry the experience acquired in this way will quickly develop an instinct for hunting in other places where scent of rats or other vermin exists.   For river hunting an experienced dog is advisable as a tutor but don't give a puppy its first lessons when the weather is cold ; wait until it is warm, as I have found this makes all the difference in the world when first introducing young dogs to hunting the river banks.   Many Sealyhams get so expert at this work that they will dive right out of sight after a rat which they have been swimming after, and come to the surface with the rodent in their mouths.

With regard to the more serious sport of badger digging, no Sealyham should be entered until it is a year old at the very earliest, and then it should be given its first lesson towards the end of the dig.   This is to say not until digging operations have taken you to within a few feet of the badger. Then take up the other dogs and put the beginner down, and encourage him to enter the hole. If he hesitates do not under any circumstances try to force him. I have seen men on more than one occasion forcibly push a dog into the mouth of the earth with the result that he got badly bitten by the badger, and was thus rendered useless ever after for this kind of work. The proportion of Sealyhams which make really dependable badger dogs is comparatively small and the dog which will enter a big earth, hunt it thoroughly, and when the badger is cornered stay there for hours on end, throwing its tongue meanwhile so that the diggers may be able to locate their position by the barking, is beyond price to followers of this most fascinating sport. But, although a game hard-bitten Sealyham is a very valuable dog and is highly prized by its owner, its worth in a monetary sense is negligible compared with the high-class show specimen which frequently realizes quite fabulous prices. The popularity of the Sealyham in America is increasing daily, and nearly all the best English specimens have sooner or later been sold to the States.

For one noted dog the sum of £1,000 was paid some years ago, and this is by no means an isolated case, as, although this sum may possibly be a record, there is not the slightest doubt that many Sealyhams of both sexes previous to the date referred to and subsequently have been sold for prices closely approximating to four figures.

THE WELSH TERRIER

By WALTER S. GLYNN

The origin of the Welsh Terrier is, I think, quite clear, but whether or not it is strictly accurate, except from the point of view of long usage of the term to call him WELSH Terrier has always been a moot point with the writer. There is no doubt the black-and-tan wire-haired Terrier, now called Welsh, is the old original black-and-tan Terrier of the British Isles, probably the oldest representation of the terrier tribe, and years ago the only terrier of Great Britain.

Welshmen have always been keen sportsmen, and what they don't know about sport would not fill many pages. It is natural therefore that considering the very great ability of the subject of these lines as a working terrier, the Welshman should seize upon him whenever they got the chance, take him into their mountain homes and adopt him for good and all as their very own. Other varieties of the Terrier as we know have made their appearance in England, Scotland and Ireland, and keep on doing so, but Welshmen for at any rate a very long time would have none of them, and even the writer can remember that it was a rare thing indeed to see any but a black-and-tan or blue-and-tan or deep red or claret-coloured terrier in and about the southern parts of North Wales. The claret-coloured Welsh Terrier was to his breed what the liver-marked one is to the Fox Terrier; he was in reality a liver-marked one but quite a different colour to the liver which one occasionally gets in for example certain strains of the smooth Fox Terrier. These liver-and-red terriers were not the result of any cross, they were pure bred, and would breed the black-and-tan all right. The writer when very young used to see a fair amount of these liver-and-reds running among the black-and-tans with Hounds in Wales and in the villages, but it is a somewhat peculiar fact that they are not to be seen now at all, or at any rate, they are very seldom seen nowadays. They seem to have been bred out just as it appears the liver in the smooth Fox Terrier is not bred anything like so much at the present time as used to be the case.

Whatever his colour, the pure bred Welsh Terrier is a game, hard, tireless terrier, ready at any time to do a real day's work and keep up with Hounds whether it be hunting the otter in the cold and rocky river or the mountain fox over the difficult and dangerous mountains which abound in North Wales. It is marvellous in fact the work they will do, the keenness, cleverness and pluck they will always display. The writer has seen them in cold weather in and out of the water all day doing the work of a hound, shivering on the bank at a check, and yet ready and willing to do their work as a terrier at any moment when required, and it is no drawing-room work to mark an otter up a wet drain and stick to him, following and marking him all the time, for some of these drains go a long way inland, and it is extraordinary how small a pipe an otter can get into.

The mountain fox in Wales is a difficult animal to hunt. Hounds are at a much greater disadvantage of course than in ordinary Foxhunting. There again the Welsh Terrier sticks to his work with a rare persistence and, short legged as many of them are, will keep up with Hounds all day long and as necessity arises will keep on doing his work as Hound or Terrier.

THE WELSH TERRIER

Top. MR. A. T. MORRIS'S WELSH TERRIER KYNAM O'GAINT (DOG)
Bottom. MRS. PAINTON JONES'S WELSH TERRIER ENEUAWC O'GAINT (BITCH)

Some of these mountains are, however, very dangerous from the fact that great slabs of fallen rock lie heaped up one on top of the other on the face of the mountain, and it is sad to relate that on occasions terriers have in going after their fox been hopelessly lost by getting down some deep and narrow cavity under these slabs from which it was quite impossible for them to get back or for any human aid to rescue them. One hears at times extraordinary stories of terriers apparently lost in this way for several days and being given up for lost, crawling home in a terribly emaciated condition, having with starvation become so thin that they have been able to squeeze out through some narrow place and thus regain their freedom.

This in reality depends on whether it is a dry or wet earth in which the terrier is incarcerated. If the latter he may not survive a single night, if the former he may live for a week or more without food, and this has, as a matter of fact, happened to Welsh Terriers running with the old-established Ynysfor Otter Hounds, who also hunt the fox on the mountains, whose Master is always very keen about his terriers, and with his great knowledge, does whatever is possible to get them back. On occasions, I know he has after superhuman work, recovered his terrier alive from an earth in which he had been for a week without any chance of food or of feeding him.. On one occasion one of his terriers got lost in a large badger earth and, it being impossible to dig through to him, he had to be left. After eight days however he got out terribly thin and weak, and with his jaws severely punished by the badger, he nevertheless got over it and lived for years afterwards. An old terrier man, by name Owen Price, well known to the writer, who always had some very game Welsh Terriers and used to take them out with the Ynysfor, had more than once some of his terriers underground for more than a fortnight. He was however able to get a little food in to them occasionally and got them out alive eventually.

The Jones family, who have lived for generations at Ynysfor, among the mountains bordering on Merionethshire and Carnarvonshire, have always, certainly from as far back as 1750, owned Hounds and the black-and-tan or blue-and-tan Welsh Terriers, which goes to prove the great antiquity of the breed and shows how much older it is than the many other breeds and varieties of the terrier so prominent nowadays.

Many of the old sporting Pictures of Hunters and Hounds have as the accompanying terrier a rough or wire-haired black-and-tan, very much resembling the present day Welsh Terrier, though some, it is true, are inclined to be prick-eared or look as if they had been to a certain extent cropped.

An old picture painted on wood in the possession of the writer would appear to show that the old black-and-tan terrier was at times used as a turnspit, for the picture shows one of them by a steaming caldron of meat by the fire, though it is not quite clear whether the caldron is being turned or whether the paw is outstretched in an endeavour surreptitiously to extract some of the contents in the absence of the master.

Game and keen as the Welsh Terrier is as a rule, he is not by nature quarrelsome, and several can be worked together with much less chance of fighting among themselves than with any of the other breeds of terriers. With all his keenness he appears to keep his head and concentrate more on the work he has on hand than most of the other varieties of the terrier, some of whom, game enough all right, get so excited that their one idea is to " fix " something at once whether it be their mate or their quarry.

The Welsh Terrier has, however, one drawback when working with Hounds and especially Otter Hounds, and that is his colour, for unless care is taken to keep hounds away from the earth where he is working, a not always easy thing to do, and he happens to come out covered with mud or earth he stands a greater chance of being mistaken for the quarry than does a white terrier. More than once to the writer's knowledge a game, good terrier has unfortunately met his death in this way. Bob Bethesda, a Champion Terrier on the Bench and a wonderfully well made and coated little Welsh Terrier owned by Mr. Edmund Buckley, M.O.H., as good at work as he was on the show bench, was much to the grief of his owner pulled to pieces as he came out of an earth by his owner's Hounds some forty or more years ago, and the same thing has happened with other Packs.

The first show of Welsh Terriers was held at Pwllheli in South Carnarvonshire in the year 1885 or 1886 at which the writer was present, and a most interesting collection was on show in the three very well filled classes which were judged by two old sporting gentlemen, one from Carnarvonshire and the other from Merionethshire, who sat in two old black oak arm-chairs and had the terriers brought up one by one before them. About the same time the Welsh Terrier Club was formed by a few good sportsmen who were very keen on working terriers, and saw no reason why good looks and working qualities should not be embodied in the same animal. The majority of the material they had to work on was of course at first somewhat rough. Thick heads, undershot jaws, hound ears, large round eyes, were rather prevalent but so also were well-ribbed-up bodies, hard water-resisting coats of good colour and good bone, legs and feet, and it was quite extraordinary how soon the very able gentlemen who took the breed in hand produced good-looking terriers without serious faults. The reason of this was that some of them, notably Mr. Cledwyn Owen of Pwllheli, knew all about the pedigrees of the terriers for generations, where they came from and from where they got their good and bad points, and being excellent judges of Hunters and Hounds, they had in their mind's eye what they wanted to produce, and careful selective breeding did the rest.

Although there has never been what one may call a furore for them as a show dog, the Welsh Terrier is now certainly a popular dog in that respect both here and in America. There are some also in France, Germany, Holland and India, where they stand the climate better than most. The difficulty about them is that whether it be on account of the dominance of their colour or their ancient lineage, the fact is that if you cross them with even a white dog the issue will be black-and-tans, and that issue if bred back again to a Welsh Terrier will breed black-and-tans again. It can easily be seen, therefore, there is not much difficulty for a dishonest person who is prepared to register a faked pedigree to get a cross of Fox Terrier into the breed and exhibit impure specimens as purebred Welsh. There is, however, a distinct difference in the type of a Welsh and a Fox Terrier, which is as a rule discernible to those who really know the breed, and although this sort of thing has always acted detrimentally to the popularity of the breed it is doubtful whether such malpractices have brought much profit to the perpetrators of them, and breeders both here and in America are now much more awake in this matter than they used to be.

Fox Terrier type is not wanted in a Welsh Terrier. It is in fact an abomination just as it is in an Irish Terrier or a Sealyham. The Welsh Terrier if left alone invariably breeds absolutely true, and it is to be trusted that a fine old breed will be left alone and that anyone who dares to tinker with it shall be brought to book.

THE WEST HIGHLAND WHITE TERRIER

By MRS. CYRIL PACEY

The West Highland White Terrier is one of the oldest working dogs of Scotland, having been used for hundreds of years before we knew of him as a show dog, for hunting foxes, badgers and wild cats among the rocks and crags of the West Highlands. To be able to do this work it was essential to have a small, narrow, very active terrier, full of pluck and courage, that could jump and scramble from rock to rock, and also be able to get to the inmost recess of the lair of its quarry. There was no chance of his being dug out, or making a wider passage by scratching among the rocks that could not be moved, and anything but a very narrow, agile terrier was likely to get fast in the slits and have his ribs broken. It was found useful to have a white or cream terrier, which was more easily seen among the rocks than his sandy or grey coloured cousins. For these reasons, he had been bred for generations by many of the oldest Scottish families entirely for his pluck and ability to work.

That the breed is of very ancient parentage is proved by the fact that over 300 years ago we hear of James I of England sending to Argyleshire for six little earth doggies to be sent to France as a present to the King. In several of Sir Edwin Landseer's famous animal paintings the West Highlander is well to the fore, especially in the well-known picture " Dignity and Impudence ". There the head study of the West Highlander is particularly good, showing the keen and alert expression that is so characteristic.

We shall always feel grateful to Col. Malcolm of Poltalloch for bringing this breed before the public. They were first shown by him at Edinburgh and called Poltalloch Terriers, the strain having been in his family for many generations and kept entirely for work. It is needless to say that such an attractive little terrier made many friends, and as several other old strains came into prominence the breed was registered at the Kennel Club as West Highland White Terriers. Two Clubs were formed about 1905, the West Highland White Terrier Clubs of Scotland and of England, to promote the interest of the breed, and classes were given for them at all the leading shows. There was at once a big demand for the gay little Highlander who captured all hearts, and for a while it seemed that the original type would be quite lost and spoilt, by the tendency there was at that time to regard them as white Scottish Terriers and breed them with long, narrow heads, and low, cloddy bodies.

Fortunately the West Highlanders had many staunch friends, who worked hard not to lose the correct type and kept their dogs for work as well as to win prizes, and this did a great deal to help to retain the proper stamp. I think it would be difficult to find a more level type of terrier than the West Highland White Terrier is to-day. Except for the fact that the modern dogs are a little shorter in back, have smaller and always erect ears, are much sounder in colour, and have shorter and better-carried tails, I do not think the breed has altered very much in type during the twenty-seven years it has been shown. The present-day West Highland White Terrier is a very sound and beautiful-looking dog, who can hold his own in the show ring by winning best of all breeds at some of our largest championship shows and is still capable of doing the job for which he was originally bred. He has a short strong muzzle, broad skull, and a well-proportioned, agile body, with a thick double coat that will resist all weathers, with a cream tinge down the middle of the back which seems impossible to breed out altogether. The courage is still there, and if given the opportunity he is ready and game to tackle any thing as his forefathers did in the West Highlands of Scotland.

It will be sufficient if I condense to some extent the standard of points approved by the West Highland White Terrier Club of England. The general appearance is that of a small, game, hardy-looking terrier, possessed of no small amount of self-esteem, with a varminty appearance, strongly built, deep in CHEST and BACK RIBS, straight BACK and powerful QUARTERS on muscular LEGS, and exhibiting in a marked degree a great combination of strength and activity. The tail should be as straight as possible, carried not too gaily, and covered with hard hair, but not bushy. The SKULL should not be too broad, being in proportion to the terribly powerful JAWS. The EARS should be as small and sharp-pointed as possible, and carried tightly up, and must be absolutely erect. The EYES of a moderate size, dark hazel in colour, widely placed, with a sharp, bright, intelligent expression. The MUZZLE should not be too long, powerful, and gradually tapering towards the nose. The NOSE, roof of mouth, and pads of feet distinctly black in colour. COLOUR, pure white ; any other colour objectionable. COAT, very important, and seldom seen to perfection ; must be double-coated. The outer coat consists of hard hair, about 2 inches long, free from any curl. The under-coat, which resembles

fur, is short, soft and close. Open coats are objectionable.
Dogs to WEIGH from 14 lb. to 18 lb., and bitches from 12 lb.
to 16 lb., and measure from 8 to 12 inches at the shoulder.

The SKULL should not be too narrow, being in proportion
to his powerful JAWS, not too long, slightly domed, and gradually tapering to the eyes, between which there should be a
slight indentation or STOP, eyebrows heavy, head and neck
thickly coated with hair. EYES, widely set apart, medium in
size, dark hazel in colour, slightly sunk in the head, sharp and
intelligent. Full eyes and also light-coloured eyes are very
objectionable. The MUZZLE should be nearly equal in length
to the rest of the skull, powerful, and gradually tapering
towards the nose, which should be fairly wide. The JAWS
level and powerful. EARS are small, erect, carried tightly up
and terminating in a sharp point. The hair on them should
be short, smooth (velvety), and they should not be cut.

The NECK is muscular and nicely set on sloping shoulders.
The CHEST is very deep, with breadth in proportion to size
of the dog. The BODY is compact, straight back, RIBS deep and
well arched in upper half of ribs, presenting a flattish side
appearance ; LOINS broad and strong, hindquarters strong,
muscular and wide across the top.

Both FORE- and HINDLEGS should be short and muscular.
The shoulder-blades should be comparatively broad, and
well sloped backwards. The points of the SHOULDER-BLADES
should be closely knitted into the backbone, so that very little
movement of them should be noticeable when the dog is walk-
ing. The ELBOW should be close to the body when moving
or standing. The FORELEGS should be straight and thickly
covered with short, hard hair. The HINDLEGS should be short
and sinewy. Thighs very muscular and not too wide apart.
The hocks bent and well set in under the body. The FOREFEET
are larger than the hind ones, are round, proportionate in
size, strong, thickly padded, and covered with short, hard hair.

TAIL, 5 or 6 inches long, covered with hard hairs, no feather,
as straight as possible, carried gaily, but not curled over back.
A long tail is objectionable. On no account should tails be
docked. Movement should be free, straight and easy all
round. In the front the leg should be freely extended forward
by the shoulder. The hind movement should be free, strong
and close. The hocks should be freely flexed and drawn close
in under the body, so that when moving off the foot the body
is thrown or pushed forward with some force. Stiff, stilty
movement behind is very objectionable.

THE WEST HIGHLAND WHITE TERRIER

Top. MRS. C. PACEY'S CH. WOLVEY PEPPER (DOG)
Bottom. MISS V. F. NEWALL'S CH. RUTH OF RUSHMOOR (BITCH)

Printed in the United Kingdom by
Lightning Source UK Ltd., Milton Keynes
137268UK00001B/34-45/P